Undefeated

*The True Story of How the Family-Owned
Shepler's Mackinac Island Ferry Service Survived
and Advanced through Three Generations*

Jean R. Beach and Dr. Don Steele

authorHOUSE®

AuthorHouse™
1663 Liberty Drive
Bloomington, IN 47403
www.authorhouse.com
Phone: 1-800-839-8640

© 2014 Jean R. Beach and Dr. Don Steele. All rights reserved.

No part of this book may be reproduced, stored in a retrieval system, or transmitted by any means without the written permission of the author.

Published by AuthorHouse 10/14/2014

ISBN: 978-1-4969-4734-5 (sc)
ISBN: 978-1-4969-4733-8 (hc)
ISBN: 978-1-4969-4732-1 (e)

Library of Congress Control Number: 2014918432

Any people depicted in stock imagery provided by Thinkstock are models, and such images are being used for illustrative purposes only.
Certain stock imagery © Thinkstock.

This book is printed on acid-free paper.

Because of the dynamic nature of the Internet, any web addresses or links contained in this book may have changed since publication and may no longer be valid. The views expressed in this work are solely those of the author and do not necessarily reflect the views of the publisher, and the publisher hereby disclaims any responsibility for them.

Contents

Dedication vii
Foreword ix
Shirtsleeves to Shirtsleeves xi

Fish Boats to Speedboats 1
Mighty Mac 14
Crucial Years, New Ventures 21
Shepler's Topless 29
Dreamboats 34
Flowers on the Water 42
Delivering the Goods 47
Great Lakes Lighthouse Keepers Association 54
Shepler's Business Culture 59
Mackinaw Crossings 62
Saving the Mackinaw 68
Leading Roles 74
Joining the Shepler Crew 88
A Visit to Mackinac Island 91
Welcome on Board 93
Shepler's Champions 101
Survive and Advance 111

Appendix 135
Bibliography 137
Acknowledgments 139

Dedication

"Undefeated" is lovingly dedicated to Suzanne and Kathy Shepler.

Foreword: By Dr. Don Steele

Years ago, I saw the movie *Somewhere in Time* and loved it. I thought it was a great story of a uniquely beautiful place. *Somewhere in Time* was a fairy tale set on Mackinac Island. This book is a true "ferry tale" that centers on a family business whose survival and prosperity is closely tied to Mackinac Island.

This is the story of Shepler's Mackinac Island Ferry, a family business that faced and adapted to decades of major challenges, any one of which might have swamped a less resilient and imaginative organization. Those challenges forced each generation of the Shepler family to grow in knowledge and develop new coping skills. Throughout the years, challenges have ranged from extreme weather and topographical demands to family differences, equipment disasters, and financial crises brought on by new technologies and old enmities. Most recently, the Shepler family business fought for its financial survival after nearly seventy years of the "boom and bust" cycles so common to family-owned and family-operated businesses.

When the Shepler family faces seemingly insurmountable challenges, it galvanizes to action. With each crisis, it is "game on" for this committed and resilient family.

This book takes its readers along for a ride through the rugged history of the northern Michigan region. *Undefeated* has a message for family business owners: Working through difficult challenges can produce closer-than-ever family ties and a stronger position in the competitive marketplace of free enterprise. Through all the Shepler family has faced, it remains undefeated!

Shirtsleeves to Shirtsleeves in Three Generations

Don Steele

The year 2008 looked good for the Sheplers. For once, there were no outside problems. However, a knotty family problem was becoming more and more evident. After more than 60 years devoted to Shepler's Mackinac Island Ferry, Bill Shepler had long since reached retirement age.

Bill is the main character in this story, but he would be the first to say that his father before him and the children he sired have all played roles central to the success of the Shepler's Mackinac Island Ferry business. There are many difficulties associated with successfully transitioning through three generations of a family-owned business. In the United States of America, the familiar aphorism "Shirtsleeves to shirtsleeves in three generations" describes the propensity of family-owned enterprises to fail by the time the founder's grandchildren are to take over. It is estimated that 70 percent of family-owned businesses fail or are sold before the second generation has a chance to take over. Just 10 percent remain active, privately owned companies for the third generation to lead.

The oldest family-owned business in America is the seventh-generation Zildjian Cymbal Company of Northwood, Maryland, which was founded in 1623 in Constantinople and moved with the family to the United States in 1629. The Shepler family had the possibility of moving, like Zildjian Cymbal, to transition through its third generation and beyond.

This is where I came in. A consulting contract with the Shepler family came to me through my longtime friends Pat Doyle and Patty Janes. Pat had served as the director of the Center for Leisure Services at Central Michigan University and, in 1969, created a CMU student internship program that would provide summer employment opportunities for Central Michigan University students all around the world. Dr. Janes succeeded Pat and continued running the program after Pat became a lobbyist. Many of the students placed through this program served over multiple summers, and some earned status as full-time employees. Others moved on to work with Disney World and other employers.

I had served as a guest lecturer for many classes of aspiring CMU students. One morning, I received a call from Pat and Dr. Janes. The purpose of their conference call was to ask me if I would be interested in taking on a consulting assignment designed to facilitate the successful transition of the Sheplers' family-owned business from the second to the third generation. Dr. Janes told me that Bill had been talking with his family about possibly retiring. Pat and Dr. Janes believed that I had the right personality and skill set to help Bill complete a successful transfer.

Doyle, Dr. Janes, and I met with Bill and his oldest son, Chris Shepler, at a restaurant in Mt. Pleasant, Michigan. Bill Shepler immediately impressed me as a charismatic, robust man who surely looked much younger than his seventy-eight years. If determination is his hallmark, laughter is his signature. Chris showed a great resemblance to his father, sharing his sandy hair and ready laughter, yet is a bit taller in stature. We had a very open exchange, and I agreed to work with the family up to and through the transition.

I recognized early on that Bill was not completely ready to step down (or even slow down), and this opinion was validated when Chris, referring to his father relinquishing the CEO role, openly voiced, "I'll believe it when I see it."

Dr. Janes had informed me that this was a strong, hardworking family with clearly defined business roles. Bill was serving as president and CEO and was stationed at the Mackinaw City dock. Chris was serving as Vice President and was stationed at the St. Ignace dock. Bill's daughter, Patty, was in charge of accounting, and his younger son, Billy, was serving as fleet captain. All of Bill's children had grown up with the business and were experienced and competent in executing their responsibilities.

Over the next year I conducted many coaching sessions with the Shepler family, individually and as a team. While my overall goal was to facilitate the transition, my experience told me that the real challenge of such transitions resides in minds and hearts of those involved. We worked together in addressing the philosophical and psychological domains related to building shared purpose and values. We engaged the family members and other Shepler's leaders in commitment-based conversations. We focused on the importance of nurturing the physical, emotional, mental, and spiritual energy of the entire staff to ensure that all employees bring focus and energy to the job each day so that they produce value. Of greatest importance was working through the emotional issues that are endemic to family-run businesses.

Helping the Sheplers successfully make the transition was a challenge because Bill Shepler had been talking about turning the reins over to his children for ten or more years. In one of our more intimate coaching sessions I asked Bill this question: "What is keeping you from retiring?"

His heartfelt response was, "I think I will die if I do!"

The key challenge in facilitating a successful transition was resolving this tension between Bill's reluctance to retire and his children's readiness to take over the daily operations of the business. While Bill's children all shared the belief that they were ready and able to take over, their "spirit of intent" regarding this potential transition was very positive and empathetic. Chris, Patty, and Billy hold deep affection for their father, and none of them wanted to force Bill's retirement against his will. They recognized that the Shepler's Mackinac Island Ferry Service was a vital and integral part of their father's life.

A second issue related to the transition was to emphasize to the new leadership team the importance of maintaining the respect of long-time employees. Having already grown up enjoying the fruits previous generations' labor carries little weight when it comes to moving the business forward. Additionally, I gave special attention to the challenges associated with Bill's combined boss and father roles. An important part of this effort was establishing regular team meetings wherein personal and business plans and issues could be openly discussed and addressed.

Finally, we wanted to anchor the family's understanding of the history of those who founded and built the Shepler's family business, the challenges these business pioneers encountered and overcame, and the emergence of a thriving community from what had once been the wilderness. The "survive and advance" attitude of the people of this region is characteristic of Michigan's historic resilience and perseverance in the face of seemingly insurmountable challenges.

While it must be recognized that Michigan faces continuing challenges, it must also be recognized that it is one of the most beautiful and diverse states in America. The "Pure Michigan" campaign promotes these qualities. The movie *Somewhere in Time,* filmed at the Grand Hotel on Mackinac Island, is still celebrated in October. The magnificent Mackinac Bridge is a spectacular sight where the ferries run back and forth and Lakes Michigan and Huron intersect. St. Ignace is a unique little town with a compelling history of its own, as is the Village of Mackinaw City.

As I learned more about the Shepler family's struggles to survive and grow over several decades, I suggested to Bill that this family-owned business might be a rare, but enlightening example of how a business successfully transitions though three generations and manages to survive and advance. I suggested that a book recording those triumphs and troubles would not only be a valued historical document but also a reminder of the importance of nurturing family relationships.

Running a family-owned business has never been harder. It is necessary to attract new markets, cope with accelerating shifts in technology, adopt new business models, face threats from competition, and cope with family-related issues and conflicts. Fully understanding the history and context of each generation is helpful in garnering the necessary courage to "keep on keeping on."

When I contacted Jean Beach and asked her if she would be interested in coauthoring the book, she quickly agreed. Jean has a deep knowledge of Michigan history and has honed her craft as a writer over many years. She has written several books. We discovered, in our early conversations about this effort, that Bill and Jean had attended Ohio Wesleyan University at the same time, although they didn't really know each other back then.

Jean and I became a team. We researched, interviewed, wrote, edited, and rewrote. She joined me on several trips to Mackinaw City as we learned about the family and the business. Bill, Chris, and Billy Shepler ferried us to Mackinac Island and St. Ignace. We visited tourist sites, ate fudge, and gained insights into the history and culture of this unique part of the United States of America. Bill took me on a lighthouse tour that was started by his friend Dick Moehl.

On other occasions, my business partner and friend Bob Bordeaux treated me to tours of some of the beautiful lakes and quaint communities that offer tourists and residents such beauty and recreational opportunity in both the lower and upper peninsulas of the great state of Michigan.

As we toured these magnificent areas of Michigan, I knew that in addition to tracking the evolution of the Shepler's family business, this book must include important historical and cultural information that brings light to the area's rare combination of beauty and harsh weather conditions.

Fish Boats to Speedboats

The *Alma F.* was the first Shepler boat. She was a humble fish boat, and William Henry Schepler probably wasn't her first owner. He was a fisherman back in the days when the Straits area teemed with whitefish, trout, and walleyes. There were so many fish that the Indians described the Straits area as "the birthplace of all fishes." William's son, also named William Henry, but nicknamed Cap, recalled working for his father. He started by cleaning fish and casting gill nets from the *Alma F.* Back around the turn of the century, a Straits fisherman built his dock by constructing boxes of eight-foot cedar logs. The boxes were floated out into the harbor and arranged in a straight line ten to twelve feet apart. Then each box was filled with stones and sunk. More cedar logs were used to attach the boxes, and planks were nailed on top to form the deck. In the winter, Cap worked with his father, cutting ice and storing it in their ice house, packed in sawdust, for sale to the railroads and the local butcher shops.

Then, when Cap was fourteen, his father bought their first little boat, and they both worked aboard her. Cap recalled, "An old Indian fisherman and I used to run a trap net rig. In the summers, we'd catch tons of fish and sell them to retail and wholesale places."

Ken Teysen, who owns Teysen's Gift Shop in Mackinaw City, knew the original William and describes work aboard a fish boat: "It was so cold that the men had to wear long johns most of the year. Their hands took a beating from constantly handling the wet, cold, heavy nets: they were arthritic and deformed."

Cap told Ken about one terrifying adventure. He was on board, dressed in boots and slicker, when he suddenly fell overboard. He wasn't missed for half an hour. "I just waited for my dad to pick me up," said Cap. "I knew he would." Cap's dad drove the *Chief Wawatam*, the railroad ferry that ran between Mackinaw City and St. Ignace. Because the *Chief* was a railroad ferry, she had to run year-round, requiring her to break through ice. She was designed as an ice-breaker, using the latest technology of the time that had been developed in the Straits of Mackinac. The *Chief Wawatam* was nicknamed "The Bull of the Woods" because she had two very powerful steam engines. William Henry also was captain of the *Algomah II*, the ferry that carried passengers and freight between Mackinaw City and Mackinac Island. The ferry service was started in 1881 by "Hap" Arnold, using the *Algomah I*, the predecessor of the *Algomah II*.

The *Algomah II* was two hundred feet long, went nine to ten miles an hour, and was powered by a three-stage steam engine that was stoked with coal. Henry Ford was said to have installed the engine. Certainly, when the *Algomah II* was retired, Ford took the engine to Greenfield Village.

At that time, the *Algomah I's* superstructure was cut off, and the old ferry was turned into a barge. Eventually, it was sunk to protect the shoreline. Then when the Mackinac Bridge was being built, concrete contractor

Merritt-Chapman and Scott built their dock over the barge. Today, Shepler's main office is located on that dock right above the *Algomah I*. Cap got his first lessons in navigation and seamanship aboard his father's fish tug and drove the *Algomah II* himself as well as being wheelsman on the *Chief* and the state boats. Frank Davis, who was an engineer on the *Algomah II,* described Cap as "a good skipper and a good brother to work with." Cap's real brother, Bob Schepler, worked as captain on the *George A. Sloan* lake freighter and kept the original spelling of the family name.

In 1930, Cap married Margaret Jamison. Ken Teyson knew the Jamisons and all their many children. Margaret, nicknamed Marge, who was the oldest, a woman described by all who knew her as dynamic and

feisty. She and Cap made a complementary pair, each bringing character traits that were vital to their marriage and the success of their business. Cap was easygoing and charming, a hard worker who played just as hard. Marge's youngest sister, Ellen Eastman, who was a flower girl at their wedding, says, "Marge always had a lot of energy; she knew what she wanted and went after it. She was the backbone of the business." About Cap, Ellen said, "He didn't know an enemy, and he never met a stranger."

After their marriage, Cap and Marge moved to Wyandotte, downriver from Detroit, because Cap got a job as captain of the *Barbette,* a big, beautiful yacht that belonged to the Hiram Walker distillery family of Windsor, Ontario. Bill remembers his dad telling him about working aboard the *Barbette*. "Everything was shined, polished, cleaned, and scrubbed. The people wanted these jobs to be just perfect. It was the culture of that area." A well-stocked liquor cabinet was in the forepeak of *Barbette*. When they went from Canada to the American shore, they had to go through customs, but they didn't declare the stock on board. It seems that Cap knew a friendly customs inspector with a taste for fine Canadian whiskey. One day, Cap slipped him the usual bottle, and the official carefully tucked it into his back pocket. As the two walked down the gangplank, the officer slipped and fell on his back. He cautiously reached around, felt something wet, and said, "God—I hope that's blood!"

Later, Cap became captain of the *Alice F.*, another big, beautiful yacht belonging to the Fisher family of Detroit's famous Fisher Body Company. The *Alice F.* had ten or twelve staterooms, and Cap headed a crew of two deck hands, a chef, two busboys, and a chief engineer. She was built of mahogany and teak with a white-painted hull and every luxury. Bill remembers one of his dad's favorite stories. "One afternoon, they were at Harbor Beach, preparing for an afternoon cocktail cruise. Dad was apprehensive about the weather. At the time, the only way to predict weather was to look at the sky and the barometer. Dad could read them well. Fishermen are on the water all the time and learn all the signs. Dad didn't like the looks of the clouds, and when he tapped the barometer, it dropped abruptly. He knew they were in for a bad blow. He got all the lines tied to the dock and even put the anchor line out. But A. J. Fisher was determined to go and insisted that they leave on schedule. Dad said, 'You go if you want to; I'm staying onshore.' Fisher was furious. The wind came up at hurricane force. It was blowing so hard that four of the lines snapped, but they stayed safely tied to the dock. When it was all over, A.J.'s father, Walter, told his son, 'Whatever Captain Shepler says, you believe. It's gospel.'"

Cap could take the Fishers wherever they wanted to go. His captain's license was for all the waters of the Great Lakes and their tributaries, and he had an ocean offshore amendment, so he could take the boat to Florida.

When World War II broke out, Cap enlisted in the Merchant Marine and served aboard the *Sultana*, a six-hundred-foot lake freighter. Cap worked four hours on and four off with very little time on shore. Years later, Bill went aboard a replica of a freighter like the *Sultana* and was appalled by the cramped and Spartan living quarters. He added, "And there was nobody there to help you in a storm."

At home, Marge raised their two children, William Richard, born in 1932, and Penny, born in 1937. Contributing to the war effort, as did most Americans, Marge planted a victory garden, had a flock of leghorn hens, and made all the children's clothes. Bill remembers that when a rubber band broke, she would tie it together instead of reaching for a new one.

After the war was over, Cap saw freighters and private yachts being scrapped and decided that Lake shipping wasn't a very promising career, especially for a man with a family. In the spring of 1945, Cap was discharged from the Merchant Marine and became the captain of the *Algomah II*, which was running between Mackinaw City and Mackinac Island. Marge, who had stayed back in Wyandotte, decided to visit Cap, whom she hadn't seen in a couple of months. While they were together there, they began to see potential consistent with their business and personal interests and talents. Cap was driving the *Algomah II*, young Bill was parking cars, and Marge had started a hot dog stand.

Bill, just twelve or thirteen, wasn't sure what his father intended to do up north. All he knew was that his father was going to find a job there and that Mackinaw City was a great place to swim. Bill and his friends would skinny dip and dive off the twenty-foothigh railroad dock. That was a great life for him. Cap moved to Mackinaw City for the summer but kept the house in Wyandotte for the winter.

The once-prosperous fishing business was defunct. Deadly sea lampreys had made their way through the Welland Canal to the Great Lakes, where they adapted all too easily to fresh water. The lampreys attached themselves to healthy fish and sucked the life out of them. Eventually, the Department of Natural Resources (DNR) developed a program of poisoning the streams where the lampreys spawned, but it was almost too late; the fish population plummeted, and it took decades to recover.

Cap's dad and mother still lived in Mackinaw City, in a house near the docks where he had leased property for his fishing business from the Michigan Central Railroad. Cap took over the lease. The property was conveniently located at the foot of the railroad dock, near the state boats dock. There was room to park cars for the ferry passengers: Bill's grandfather, William, had been running a parking business on a small scale, and Cap decided to expand on the idea. He put up signs and charged thirty-five cents a day or seventy-five cents for twenty-four hours. He remodeled part of his dad's old fish net building into a home for the family with two bedrooms, bath, kitchen, and living room.

All his life, Cap was daring and took chances to succeed, but he always did so with the full backing of Marge, who thoroughly investigated and approved every project and expenditure. It was a winning combination.

Now Cap and Marge had another idea. The ferries were so slow that people waiting to cross often stood around for a long time with nothing to do. They turned the rest of the fish net building into a snack bar. She did the cooking: hamburgers and hot dogs, coffee and soft drinks, and her own baked goods. Bill's friend, Jack Kerby, remembers those pies. "They were her specialty, and the tourists really grabbed them up." Marge even planted a rhubarb patch for her rhubarb pies. She washed laundry every day and hung it by the building to dry.

Bill was put in charge of parking the cars. He was sometimes helped by friends like Jack. Bell's Fishery was next door to Shepler's new enterprise, and little Donny Bell, five years old, became Bill's shadow. He was a little guy with a speech impediment, always dressed in a cowboy outfit, who thought Bill's job waving cars into place was especially desirable. Bill finally gave into his pleadings and allowed him to give it a try. "How much do I owe you?" asked the customer.

"Firty-five cents," lisped Donny proudly. Bill and Jack cracked up.

On another day, Donny got a chance to share a rare treat. *Algomah's* freight came in on trucks or by train. One day, while they were unloading groceries for an island restaurant, two half-gallon tubs of vanilla ice cream fell into the harbor. After the Algomah crew left, Jack and Bill decided to go after them. It wasn't an easy job—the ice cream was at the bottom of the harbor, under twenty feet of water—but they finally managed to lug the tubs to the surface. Just as they were about to dig in, a woman customer gave them a chocolate cake she didn't want to take to the island. Donny Bell got a share, too, and none of them ever forgot the time they had all the vanilla ice cream and chocolate cake they could possibly eat.

Bill's memories aren't always so delicious. He used to play in an ancient sixteen-foot skiff. One day, his cousin Jim Anderson joined him, and they decided to take it out. Jim had had polio and couldn't use one arm, but that didn't stop them. Neither did the fact that they didn't have a set of oars. They decided that their one oar plus a piece of wood from an orange crate would do just fine. Their idea was to paddle out a hundred feet from the end of the dock to an old crib that had once been a part of the dock. Bill planned to grab one of the pilings to turn around and paddle back. However, the wind came up and took them much farther out. No matter how hard they paddled, they kept going farther and farther from safety. Finally, a man on shore saw their plight and came to their rescue in a leaky rowboat. Bill says ruefully, "I caught hell, and I deserved it. Jim couldn't even swim."

The parking lot and snack bar did well, and Cap came up with still another idea. He saw how it was possible to change the rather tedious forty-five-minute trip on the *Algomah II* into a swift and glamorous adventure. He remembered the quality of the yachts and envisioned a speedboat that was beautifully made and luxuriously appointed. He found a boat that had been owned by the Jefferson Beach Amusement Park. She was a twenty-eight-foot Hacker Craft with a six-cylinder Kermath engine, made of varnished mahogany with chromed hardware. The only problem was that she'd been neglected and was in sad shape. But Cap knew how to take care of a wood boat. He rebuilt the engine. He took out the screws, one at a time, and replaced them with bigger ones. He stripped off the layers of battered varnish, sanded and bleached the wood, and finished it with ten coats of fresh varnish. The hardware was replaced, and the leather seat cushions were recovered. The boat had new red carpeting, and a red carpet on the dock led to the boat. Cap and Marge named her *Miss Penny* for their daughter. Bill's friend Hap Dowler remembered her, "The *Miss Penny* was really fast; her top speed was thirty-five miles per hour, but she wasn't too good in rough water."

With the boat in beautiful shape, Cap and Marge worked out the details of their ferry service. The *Algomah II* made only five trips a day to the island. Cap could see that there was a real opening for a charter service that was completely flexible. Their customers would be people who had missed the last departure at 6:45 p.m. or needed immediate service. They

ran charters at all hours, charging $12 for a boatload in the daytime and $15 at night. Mackinaw City businessman Stan McRae recalled the early days: "Shepler's would operate when other boats quit. I wonder how many hours (Cap) logged."

Bill says, "We'd go out when Arnold's was still tied to the dock—but safety always comes first. If we think it's not safe, we don't operate."

David Armour, deputy director of Mackinac State Historic Parks, crossed about three days a week for thirty-six years and began crossing with Cap. He says, "Cap was more interested in getting people aboard than running on a schedule. If a regular was late, he'd wait for him. I'd ask when the boat was going and Mrs. Shepler would read the schedule, but I'd say 'But when is it *really* going to leave?'"

Bill said, "It was tough. Mom cooked, Dad ran the speedboat, and I parked cars."

When Bill was sixteen, Cap encouraged him to get his captain's license. He had the necessary 365 four-hour days of experience working with his father, and Cap coached him on the questions he was likely to get. Before WWII, Cap had spent five days in Detroit's Federal Building, taking his captain's license tests that covered trigonometry, buoyancy, navigation, and a host of other information, so he had a good idea of what Bill would be up against. Bill took the test in St. Ignace, passed, and became one of the youngest captains on the Lakes.

At the time, Bill's real passion was football. With the ferry service running into October, Bill went down to Wyandotte in September and stayed so he could play for Roosevelt High. His aunt, Ellen Eastman, remembers that Bill ate and slept the game, was absolutely determined to win, and even yelled football plays in his sleep.

Bill graduated from high school in 1950 and started college at Ohio Wesleyan University in Delaware, Ohio, where he joined Phi Gamma Delta fraternity, participated in AROTC, and played football. Jack Kerby, a couple of years older than Bill, was a Phi Gam at OWU and encouraged Bill to go there and to join his fraternity. He remembers Bill as "a great guy, energetic and athletic."

Another fraternity brother, Hap Dowler, played football with Bill and describes him as "a guard and a good one … a good-looking scamp with an ever-present smile who always had something nice to say." Hap added, "He was just an average student, but in the real world, he knew how to make it work." The "prepare and persevere" coaching Bill got as he played football would be reflected in his future on-the-job performance.

"I've never seen anyone with better people skills," said Hap, and he remembers Bill cutting hair in the third-floor bathroom of the Fiji house at fifty cents a head.

The friendships he formed in high school and at OWU have lasted. Some of those friends worked with him in the summer and lived with him in the Palace, an old net shed near Bell's Fishery that Bill and Hal Williams turned into a makeshift dorm. They put up cardboard partitions, installed a shower and a heater, and painted the place with dribs and drabs of leftover paint, resulting, they hoped, in an interesting rainbow effect. Friends Noel Bufe and Hap were also Palace residents over the years and remember it as primitive but fun. Hap says, "We parked cars and handled luggage, and sometimes we got tips. But there were some people who parked in the lot and didn't pay. We'd jack up their cars and put blocks under their rear ends." They worked seven days a week, but they found time to run on the beach and play tennis. Hap describes Bill's dad as "portly, with a great sense of humor. He worked hard and was a good troubleshooter on the boats."

Cap had to be an imaginative mechanic. One time, he was coming from the island when the Corps of Engineers was dredging. During that operation, the current was so strong that the buoys marking the channel between Round Island and Mackinac Island were forced underwater. Cap ran over the buoys, wiped out a propeller, and tore out a strut, leaving six 5/8-inch holes through the hull which immediately started taking on water. They had to be plugged, but what with? Cap grabbed the dipstick he used to measure the fuel in the gas tank. He pushed it into the first hole and found it fit exactly, so he snapped it off, repeated the operation on the other five holes, stopped the leaks, and saved the boat.

Of Bill's mother, Hap says, "She was the brains of the business."

Noel Bufe played football in high school with Bill and also summered in the Palace. He appreciated how the Sheplers included him in family activities. "My mother died early, and I got to watch a family with a mother. It influenced my life. Mrs. Shepler had this uncanny ability to know everything that was going on. We called her Hawkeye." Of Cap, Noel said, "He expected a lot, and he inspired us to do well, even in our personal lives."

Now that there were two captains in the family, the Sheplers could use two boats and expand the service. A friend of Cap's was running another charter service but wanted to get out of the business. Cap bought his thirty-foot Hacker speedboat, and they named it *Fiji* for Bill's fraternity. The *Fiji* was long and narrow, good in rough weather. Bill and his friends used the *Fiji* for water skiing when they were coming back empty from the island. The trip made a good workout.

An unexpected source of charters was crew members from freighters who had missed their boats in Erie, Detroit, or Chicago. They would drive up to Mackinaw City and charter Shepler's to take them out and put them aboard. Bill remembers, "There was quite a trick to it. Dad or I would run them out alongside, and the freighter crew would lower a ladder so they could climb aboard. It was tricky because those freighter captains wouldn't slow down for anything. We'd maneuver alongside, being careful to stay far enough away so we wouldn't run into the freighter's steel hull. One time, I had to put a captain's wife aboard. I don't know why she missed the boat, and for a little while, I didn't think she'd make it up the ladder. The captain didn't slow down, even for her. I always wondered if he was secretly hoping she'd fall in the drink."

Bill also remembers a regular customer. "He was a crusty old judge from Chicago who arrived Friday night in a big car driven by a chauffeur. I don't know why he went to Mackinac Island every weekend, and of course, I never asked. One night, it was really rough: the wind was howling, and there were big waves with whitecaps. I didn't think he'd come, but he turned up as usual, all set to go. The chauffeur didn't want to go. He said he'd stay with the car, but the judge wouldn't hear of it and ordered him to get into the boat. About halfway across, I looked around. The judge was in his usual seat, but the chauffeur had vanished. At first, I thought he'd fallen overboard, but then I noticed a pile of rain gear in the bottom of the *Fiji*. It was moving. The chauffeur was hiding under them and praying as loud as he could."

Even the competition sometimes chartered Shepler speedboats. One foggy night, Arnold's had more passengers from Mackinac Island to St. Ignace than they could handle, so they called on Cap and Bill. "Dad took ten in the *Miss Penny*, and I took ten in the *Fiji*. I followed Dad's tail light in the fog so I wouldn't hit him, but when we were seven or eight miles into the trip, I heard an odd sound, and I started losing power. I had the throttle wide open, but I was only getting half speed. Then I lost Dad. We didn't have radios back then, so I couldn't let him know what was going on. I was going slower and slower. And then I saw the light from St. Ignace. The engine completely quit, but luckily I glided into the dock with my passengers. Dad had to tow me back; I'd blown a piston."

Bill could have used modern equipment on another foggy crossing. "I was about seventeen or eighteen and was taking a couple of Indiana schoolteachers from the Island to Mackinaw City. The only navigational instruments I had to keep course were my watch for running time and an old car compass for direction. The problem with the compass was that it twirled around with every wave. I got an occasional reading, and of course I know how long it would take to go the distance. That's all I had to find my way in the fog. The two teachers were absolutely terrified. When the time was up, I found us in five feet of water, but I didn't know where. We could have been near Boblo Island or maybe the Lower Peninsula or even the U.P. I slowed the boat, took a chance, and hugged the shore, looking for something familiar. There were big rocks below and then—Mackinaw City! Mildred and Florence were mightily impressed. They came back year after year and told their adventure again and again. I became a bigger hero with every telling. But those teachers never knew that I was just as scared as they were!"

Over the years, things improved. Bill says, "By the early fifties, we had radios on board, but they weren't anything like the radios we have today. They were big, heavy things with vacuum tubes. One time, a wire in the radio shorted out and blue smoke rolled out. When I went back and pulled up the hatch cover, I saw a flame crackling along the wire. Ed Curtis, a mechanic, just happened to be on board, and he cut the burning wire, extinguishing the fire. But a woman on board with a little child panicked and tried to get out. Since we were in the middle of the Straits, I asked her where she thought she was going. All she could say was that they were getting off the boat. I finally got her calmed down, and she didn't get off until we docked in Mackinaw City. I realized then that people can do some pretty crazy things if they get panicked, and I realized that it's important for the captain and crew to be well-trained so they can handle emergencies." Today's ferries are equipped with global positioning systems, the latest marine radios, radar, and gyroscopic compasses, and the crews are painstakingly trained to handle just about any emergency.

The speedboats were fast and fun, but they were always breaking down. Bill says, "You were all by yourself with just an oar to paddle in." By the nature of their business, they had to run in all kinds of weather, fog, and heavy seas. The speedboats just weren't built for six- or seven-foot waves. They decided that they needed a two-engine boat with a roof over their heads.

In 1949, the Sheplers bought a thirty-foot Bay Craft kit boat from Bay City. She had two V8 engines and carried twenty-four people. The kit consisted of lumber, the oak ribs, and a plan. Cap put her together in Cheboygan that winter. The new boat was named *Miss Margy*, in honor of Mrs. Shepler. A new boat was not the only change that would affect the Sheplers.

Mighty Mac

Throughout his college career, Bill came home every summer to work with his dad. In 1954, he graduated from college and that September he joined the Air Force to fulfill his ROTC obligation. He started at Lackland Air Force Base in Texas for basic training and then went on to maintenance school in Rantoul, Illinois. Most of his Air Force years were spent doing airplane maintenance and repair at George Air Force Base in California.

1954 was also the year that construction started on the Mackinac Bridge. It had been a long time coming. In 1888, one year after the Michigan Central's Grand Hotel opened, railroad baron Cornelius Vanderbilt announced, "We now have the largest, well-equipped hotel of its kind in the world. Now what we need is a bridge across the Straits."

Vanderbilt's proposal was only wishful thinking: everyone knew that it was impossible to build a bridge uniting Michigan's two peninsulas. What about that turbulent winds and waves in that area? What about the water? It was hundreds of feet deep. What about the crushing build-up of ice? What about the length of such a bridge? Nobody had ever attempted to build a bridge five miles long. And, as late as the 1850s, Washington DC regarded the northern Great Lakes as impossibly remote. When the Soo Canal was proposed, powerful Senator Henry Clay called the Soo, "As beyond the remotest settlement of the United States, if not the moon."

The success of the Brooklyn Bridge, dedicated in 1883, encouraged backers of a Mackinac Bridge, but the Brooklyn Bridge, wonder though it was, didn't present as many serious problems.

Over the years, other solutions were tried. In 1881, three railroads, the Michigan Central, the Grand Rapids and Indiana, and the Detroit Mackinac and Marquette got together to form the Mackinac Transportation Company. It operated a railroad ferry across the Straits named the Chief Wawatam which could carry twenty-one railroad cars. The Wawatam was joined by a smaller boat, the Santa Maria, which carried eleven railroad cars and was equipped with two screws aft and one forward. They ran between their own docks in Mackinaw City and St. Ignace. Both were powerful ice-crushers. Modern-day technologies of crushing ice were developed by a captain from St. Ignace in the 1800s.

A floating tunnel was suggested in 1920 by Horatio Early, Michigan's first state highway commissioner, but the idea was quickly shot down. With more and more automobiles coming into use, in 1923 the legislature ordered the state to establish ferry service for autos across the Straits. The state boats, which all carried cars, passengers and some cargo, were the Mackinaw City, the City of Munising, the City of Petoskey, the Sainte Ignace, the City of Cheboygan, and the Straits of Mackinac. Even running around the clock, the ferries could only handle nine thousand cars a day. In peak times, such as the start of hunting season, cars would be backed up to Cheboygan, sixteen miles from Mackinaw City.

In 1929, a feasibility study was made. Engineers estimated that a bridge would cost $30 million, an impossible sum. Even if the money had been available, some engineers still doubted that the bridge could be built.

In 1934, in the depths of the Depression, an attempt was made to take advantage of the New Deal's Public Works Administration, which was funding public building programs of all kinds. Governor William Comstock established a Mackinac Bridge Authority. Prentiss Brown was the authority's legal counsel; the bridge would become his lifelong passion. Charles E. Fowler, a prominent New York bridge engineer, was hired to draw up the plans. He envisioned a series of causeways and bridges from Cheboygan to Bois Blanc to Round Island, across the western tip of Mackinac Island to St. Ignace. The Bridge Authority hoped to get loans and grants from the PWA, but they were turned down.

Figuring that the complicated Fowler plan was responsible for their failure, the Bridge Authority hired Francis McMath and James Cissell to draw up plans for a span that went directly from Mackinaw City to St. Ignace. They were turned down again, despite the fact that this time, they had the backing of the Army Corps of Engineers and President Franklin D. Roosevelt.

Still another try was made in 1937 when Murray D. Van Wagoner was highway commissioner. The bridge was designed by Leon Moiseeif. Perhaps it was good thing that his bridge was never built: he was the designer of the notorious Tacoma Narrows Bridge, "Galloping Gertie," that collapsed in 1940. However, a million-dollar causeway was built as the northern approach to the bridge, reaching a mile into the Straits from St. Ignace. World War II put an end to further planning "for the duration."

In 1948, G. Mennen Williams ran for governor, promising to revive the bridge project. The Mackinac Bridge Authority was reestablished in 1951. They announced the results of still another feasibility study by three of the world's foremost long-span bridge engineers. They determined that the bridge was a go from all standpoints: engineering, financial, and economic. It would be financed by revenue bonds without any cost to the taxpayers. Tolls would pay for its maintenance.

Some legislators bitterly opposed the bridge bill. They were joined by the State Highway Department, which had just spent $4.5 million on a huge new ferry, the Vacationland.

Prentiss Brown, who would be known as "the father of the bridge," Charles T. Fisher, and Grand Hotel owner W. Stewart Woodfill worked with Governor Williams to sell the bridge to legislators and the bankers and investors who would buy the bonds.

This time, David B. Steinman was chosen to design the bridge. As a boy, he had sold newspapers in the shadow of the Brooklyn Bridge and told friends, "Someday, I'm going to build a bridge like that!" His friends laughed at him. Dr. Steinman's company had been involved in building over four hundred bridges on five continents, but the Mackinac Bridge would be his crowning achievement. A staff of 350 engineers worked with him on the plans, turning out eighty-five thousand blueprints. The bridge was designed to be super-safe, able to withstand wind velocities up to six hundred miles per hour. It would cost a total of $96,400,033.33.

Merritt-Chapman and Scott won the contract to build the concrete substructure. Most of their work isn't visible: two-thirds of the finished bridge is underwater. Merritt-Chapman began by building a breakwater and dock at the foot of Main Street. They needed to load their boats with the 466,300 cubic yards of concrete used in the bridge.

The American Bridge Division of U.S. Steel got the contract for the steel superstructure, and 2,500 workers poured into Mackinaw City, turning a quiet little town of nine hundred permanent residents into a boom town. It was the greatest bridge construction team ever assembled. The jobs were dangerous. Divers wore cumbersome suits, lead shoes, and heavy brass helmets, working in perilous depths. Instead of carrying scuba tanks on their backs, they were fed air through hoses which could snarl, kink, and tear loose. Nitrogen poisoning, the dreaded "bends," was a constant possibility. Steel workers had to contend with icy temperatures and high winds while working on narrow beams hundreds of feet above the water. Five men lost their lives building the bridge.

Diver Frank Pepper—September 10, 1954
Welder James LeSarge—October 10, 1954
Laborer Albert Abbot—October 25, 1954
Steelworker Jack Baker—June 6, 1956
Steelworker Robert Koppin—June 6, 1956

Still another man, painter Daniel Doyle, was killed in a fall on August 7, 1997. Despite the hardships and hazards, the workers took a fierce pride in their bridge, and many looked back on the years of its construction as the best years of their lives. It had been estimated that it would take ten years to build the bridge—they did it in less than four.

Visitors came by the thousands to watch the bridge go up. Shepler's soon found that their boat trips were in great demand by the crowds who wanted a close-up view of the construction site. Another high-speed cruiser was needed to keep up with the demand. She was another Bay Craft kit boat, thirty-four feet long with an eleven-foot beam, and was powered by twin gasoline engines. Cap went down to Bay City to build her in the winter of 1953. Made of mahogany, she had the speed and style Shepler's was known for. They named her *Billy Dick* for William Richard. The speedboats and two cruisers would be filled for every trip. While the construction business was a plus for the ferry business, it did present some challenges.

Hap Dowler remembers one incident that occurred right before Bill went into the Air Force. "When the bridge was being built, they brought up pylons for the towers from Alpena. They were 200 feet long and 136 feet in diameter. To get the pylons to the Straits, they filled them with air, capped both ends, and towed them up through Lake Huron with tugs. One night, Bill and I were coming back from a charter run to the Island. We spotted a tug with a light indicating that it had a tow. Suddenly, we saw a little white light to our left that kept vanishing and reappearing, as if something moving kept blocking it ... Bill slowed down and turned on the spotlight. We were headed right for one of those floating pylons." Bill adds, "It's a miracle that we didn't hit it or run over the cable."

In that same year of 1954, the six main piers of the bridge were built. Merritt-Chapman and Scott drove enormous steel tubes called caissons right down to the bedrock nearly three hundred feet below the surface of the Straits. These were filled with reinforced concrete. The next year, they built twenty-eight more piers while American Bridge constructed the two main towers, each soaring 552 feet above the water. Then the two main cables were strung. Each main cable is 25.25 inches in diameter. In all, forty-one thousand miles of cable were used, along with 71,300 tons of structural steel and millions of steel rivets and bolts. In 1957, the main suspension span linked the two sides of the bridge and the roadway was paved. Finally, the whole bridge was painted, first with red lead primer and then with its signature green and cream colors. When University of Michigan fans objected to the color scheme, the bridge changed its night lights to maize and blue.

The Mackinac Bridge crosses three times as much water as the Golden Gate. Its total length is five miles, and the suspension span is 8,614 feet. For forty- one years, it was the longest suspension span in the world. In 1988, it was surpassed by both Japan's Pearl Bridge and the Great Belt Bridge in Denmark.

When the bridge opened on November 1, 1957, Gov. Williams led a cavalcade of cars across the bridge. It included David Steinman and Prentiss Brown, members of the Bridge Authority, fifty members of the Michigan legislature, and 150 newspapermen, plus representatives from the Associated Press, United Press International, *Life* magazine, and radio station WJR, Detroit. There was also a car from every county in the Upper Peninsula.

The official dedication was held on the weekend of June 25–27, 1958. It was the biggest celebration Michigan has ever seen, before or since. The main events were in Mackinaw City, St. Ignace, and Cheboygan but Petoskey and Sault Ste. Marie joined in with festivities of their own. There were military displays, parades with floats and bands, and queens from all over Michigan. There were Indian ceremonies, fireworks, vessels ranging from birch bark canoes to the Coast Guard icebreaker *Mackinaw*, and lots and lots of speeches. Prentiss Brown was master of ceremonies for the formal dedication, and just as the festivities ended, Mother Nature stepped in and produced a grand finale in the form of a raging storm.

On Labor Day of 1958, Governor Williams began a tradition that continues to this day when he led a group of pedestrians across the bridge from St. Ignace to Mackinaw City. Since then, every governor has led the Labor Day walk, which attracts sixty to seventy thousand hikers. It's a must for politicians and the only time that pedestrians are allowed on the bridge. Some participants choose to run. Unlike walkers, who only have to show up, runners have to be pre-qualified and preregistered. Also, every year, about twenty-five hardy souls turn up to swim the distance. Shepler's has a special "Ride the Boat to Walk the Bridge" service on Labor Day. Prospective hikers are ferried from Mackinaw City to the island and then to St. Ignace, where shuttles take them to the bridge.

Since the bridge opened, a steady stream of cars, trucks, campers and RVs have crossed the bridge. In 1998 the hundred millionth bridge toll was recorded. It was a cyclist named Dan Gilment on his Harley.

Some interesting people and vessels have crossed *under* the bridge, including a few planes with foolhardy pilots. In 1959, the royal yacht *Brittania* steamed under with Queen Elizabeth II and Prince Philip out on deck. The bridge marks the last bit of the Chicago to Mackinac race; the sailboats pass under the bridge just before they reach the island. Crews and passengers on freighters, private boats, tall ships, cutters, and ferries have looked up at the bridge. From any angle, the Mackinac Bridge is simply spectacular.

Crucial Years, New Ventures

Bill came home from the Air Force in time to celebrate the opening of the bridge, and he didn't come alone. In California, he met a lovely young woman, Suzanne Mallagh. Sue, a native of San Luis Obispo, was working as a secretary for the Federal Service Finance Corporation in San Francisco.

According to Bill, "While in the Air Force, none of us wanted to live in the barracks on the base. I moved off base with a fellow pilot, Bob Brockman. We had an apartment in Apple Valley, California. Jack Sears lived in the same complex. He was managing the Apple Valley Inn that included a golf course and lounge. We became great friends. Jack's wife, Sidney, worked in San Francisco, and she was a good friend of Suzanne Mallagh. One day Jack said, 'Sidney is coming to Modesto and is bringing a friend. Would you like to join us for the weekend?' Jack wanted to fly there, and I said 'absolutely!'"

Bill went over to the air base and checked out two flight suits for himself and Jack. On Saturday afternoon, they left for Modesto, about a ninety-minute flight. The plane they were flying was a PT Primary Trainer. It had an open cockpit and was fully stressed for aerobatics.

When they arrived at the Modesto airport, Sidney and Suzanne were waiting. Bill says, "I saw this stunning brunette in front of me. I asked her if she would like to go for a flight, and she accepted my invitation. I strapped her in with the seat belt, shoulder straps, and parachute. I told her that her job, to get us started, was to pull the stick back to her belly and hold it there. Then I set the right fuel mixture for the throttle and set the brakes. Because there is no starter, I had to pull the propeller to start the engine. As the engine started, I hopped in the plane, took over the stick from Suzanne, and released the brakes, and we took off. We got to about two thousand feet. We were wearing helmets and goggles with earphones inside the helmet. I called Suzanne on the intercom and asked her if she would mind if we did a few maneuvers. She said, 'Fine'.

Bill says, "I started slowly with a lazy eight, a chandelle, and a minor stall. Inspired by this good-looking gal sitting next to me, I got this grand inspiration to do a loop. With this aircraft, I had to dive the plane to get 160 knots of air speed. The secret, then, was to pull the plane back gently and let it fly itself through the loop using the air speed I had generated through the dive. Undoubtedly excited about Suzanne, I was a little abrupt with the stick. I flew the airplane into a vertical position where it lost air speed. At that moment, lacking airspeed, the plane fell backwards out of the sky. The plane was dropping backward toward earth, putting tremendous stress on the control surfaces, especially the elevator. This caused the airplane to flip violently, nose down.

"The movement was so violent and so quick that all of the candy and gum wrappers and stuff under the floorboards flew up into our faces. The airplane lost fuel (gravity feed, no fuel pump). This caused the engine to quit. I had to continue the dive in order to generate enough air speed to possibly glide to a landing. As I looked for a space to land, the air pressure against the propeller caused it to turn, and the engine kicked in. It didn't take me long to land the plane. As we were climbing out, Suzanne looked at me and said, 'That was fun, do you do that often?'"

Little did Suzanne know that this flight would mirror life with Bill Shepler. They were married on May 16, 1958 in Wyandotte, Michigan.

"I'm Catholic," says Sue. "Bill went to a Methodist college, we were married by a Baptist minister, and I taught in a Presbyterian-Methodist Sunday school, so you could say we're pretty well-rounded."

Bill and Suzanne came back to a discouraging situation: the business was in deep trouble. An expert skier, Bill took a second job as ski instructor at Boyne Mountain in the winter. The rest of the year, he worked with Cap and Marge. Housing was hard to find in both Mackinaw City and Boyne Mountain, so Bill and Suzanne bought a trailer and located it on the Shepler dock, behind the office in Mackinaw City. This allowed Bill to be close to both of his places of employment while his family was right there with him.

Bill says, "With the completion of the new Mackinac Bridge that connected the lower and upper peninsulas, we found that Shepler's didn't have much to celebrate. Now that people could drive across the new bridge, the state boats that had run from Mackinaw City to St. Ignace in the Upper Peninsula were retired, thus making the state dock available. Arnold Transit quickly leased the vacated state dock. That took away most of our parking business, since now the *Algomah II* left from a dock too far from Shepler's to be convenient. That also meant there was no business at the snack bar. And there were no more cruises to look at bridge construction.

"We almost died on the vine. We were basically out of the flow of things. We had no money. We had no business. It was the low point of our family business—I felt helpless and sick. This was the lowest point in Shepler's quest to stay in business. I couldn't sleep.

"The whole summer of 1958, everybody was doing great but us. Arnold's had developed diesel boats. They only went 10–11 miles per hour, but they were efficient, had a high capacity, and only needed a crew of three. Seventeen guys got together and bought the retired state boat *Straits of Mackinac* for only $25,000 and started running from the state dock in Mackinaw City to the Bay View Dock on the island. The capacity of the *Straits of Mackinac* was a thousand passengers, and it made six trips per day.

"The bus companies were making a fortune carrying passengers across the bridge and back. We talked to everyone, trying to find a way to stay in business, but everything cost money. We couldn't even afford to advertise. We had nothing to invest, and banks wouldn't loan us any money. We didn't even have a deep water location, and the lakes were low that year. I was like a drowning man looking for something—anything—to save us. I almost quit."

Because the Straits of Mackinac ferry service was in competition with Arnold Transit, they agreed to let Shepler's bring their charter boat passengers to the Straits of Mackinac dock on Mackinac Island. Shepler's was only running two charter boats at the time, but the use of the dock enabled them to increase their passenger loads. The Straits of Mackinac people were not real happy about that turn of events.

Then Shepler's got a break. According to Bill Shepler, "First, we were able to buy some waterfront property in an area of Mackinac Island that Jack Chambers had labeled 'Orphan's Corner' because there was truly nothing there. The opportunity to buy this property fell into place because our friend, Louie Yellen, owned half interest, along with Arnold Transit, in a parcel of Mackinac Island waterfront property. He asked the judge to split the property so that he would own his parcel independently. The judge agreed, and a short time later, Yellen offered to sell his parcel to us. This was vitally important because it gave us space to build our own dock instead of using the Straits Transit dock or other dock facilities on the island that we did not own."

Bill added. "The second thing we did was to build a thirty-foot stub of a dock on our newly acquired parcel of waterfront property. We had an open dock, with no break wall to protect us from weather from the east, so we were completely open to Lake Huron's wind and sea conditions. On rough weather days, with wind out of the east, passengers had to jump from the boat to the dock between waves. And on especially rough days, we couldn't operate our two little wooden charter boats at all. What we did have was our own dock and our own schedules. We also had a great crew: Cap and I drove the boats, and Mom sold tickets and cooked our meals. We were happy as clams!"

In the sixties, Shepler's built the first addition to the dock, adding two hundred feet and a break wall to protect them from the weather. While this improved things in many ways, a problem arose when the neighbor that owned the adjoining property sought a permit to build a dock within about twenty-five feet of the Shepler dock. The Sheplers fought this permit but lost. The neighbor, who just happened to be a part owner of a competitor, Star Line, built his dock, saying that it would only be used for personal yachts. However, it was soon rumored that the neighbor was going to apply for an extension to his dock. Such an extension would hinder Shepler's access to its own dock.

Sheplers then quietly applied to the Department of Natural Resources for another two-hundred-foot extension to its dock, as the state of Michigan requires. The permit, if granted, would include an additional break wall. In order to do this, Shepler's would also have to get a permit to lease the bottom land over which their dock would be built. As he drew out his plans for the dock to show the DNR people what he needed, Bill unexpectedly discovered that he could extend the amount of bottom land he wanted to lease in front of his property to include the bottom land in front of his neighbor's dock. Bill secured the permit to extend his dock, build another break wall, and leased the bottom lands in front of his dock as well as the bottom land in front of his neighbor's dock.

Throughout all of these deals, Suzanne retained her faith in Bill. Another woman might have been disappointed or even resentful of the risky business decisions and the change in their lifestyle. A trailer on a dock in northern Michigan is far from the cosmopolitan style of San Francisco, but she says, "The quarters may have been a little tight, but it was nice. I had no complaints; it was A-OK with me."

Slowly, one agonizingly small step at a time, Shepler's managed to pull out of the slump. The buses gave Bill the idea of taking people by boat to see the bridge from underneath and then taking them back by bus. He called it "Over and Under the Mackinac Wonder," and the idea caught on.

Because Merritt-Chapman and Scott had the contract for all of the bridge concrete, they built a dock right at the foot of Main Street in Mackinaw City to load barges to carry concrete to the bridge site. With the completion on the bridge, Merritt-Chapman and Scott donated the dock to Mackinaw City. Mackinaw City tried unsuccessfully to lease it, but no one was interested.

At this same time, because of low water in the Great Lakes, Shepler's could not use Cap's fish dock. Somehow Cap managed to scrape up the money to negotiate a ten-year lease with Mackinaw City at $1,000 per year.

Fortunately, Uncle Lee Brown got a stumpage contract to haul logs from Boblo to Mackinaw City. Uncle Lee, who was married to Cap's sister, Melba, was a partner in Brown Brothers Construction of Lansing, whose many projects included building overpasses on highways I-94 and I-96 in the Lansing area. He told Cap that if Cap and Bill would help in the logging enterprise, Lee would create a dock structure on the leased dock from Mackinaw City. They eagerly agreed. Lee brought up a special barge and a crane. The barge was in sections so that it could be brought up on the highways. Cap bought a thirty-foot tug from a local marine contractor and a gasoline engine. They put together the barge sections, and Bill drove the tug, towing the barge, to Boblo. They could make only one round trip a day, as the logs had to be cut and hauled to the dock. There, Bill used a forklift to load them into a barge. Bill remembers, "It was a big barge and held a lot of logs. We started early in the morning, and sometimes we wouldn't get home till late at night." It took all fall to complete the job.

Lee was as good as his word and made the dock usable for the Sheplers. Now they had a deep-water mooring, with protection from east weather, in an accessible location at the end of Main Street.

This was Shepler's first great victory. They had survived a huge challenge.

The next year, Cap built the building that now houses the Shepler offices. He originally wanted to put a restaurant on the second floor, but the Small Business Association refused to loan him the money to build the restaurant. Instead, they turned the second floor into an apartment for Cap and Marge.

Their daughter Penny had married for the first time in 1960. Tragically, she died of a brain tumor when she was only thirty-six, leaving her second husband and three small boys.

When Boyne Mountain completed its new ski area, called Boyne Highlands, Bill was promoted to the role of director of the Boyne Highlands Ski School. Bill and Suzanne moved their trailer to Harbor Springs for the winter.

Eleanor and Doug Jardine lived across the street from the Sheplers' trailer, and the two couples quickly became friends, even though the Sheplers didn't have much time for socializing. "Bill always worked long hours," says Eleanor. "They'd be having dinner about the same time we were going to bed." They did play cards and picnic, and Eleanor remembers staying with the older Shepler children when the younger ones were born.

Kathy was born in 1959, Chris in 1962, Patty in 1969, and Billy in 1971. Money was still so tight that Bill often had to get an advance from Boyne to get through November and December.

In the summer, the trailer went back to Mackinaw City. Members of the family remember that rusty trailer with nostalgia and also despair. Bill recalls, "I'd wake up very early in the morning, and if I felt the wind buckling the trailer wall by my head, I knew we wouldn't be able to run that day. People would come to the dock, and we'd have to tell them, 'We're not operating today—you'll have to take the ferry three blocks away.' We were in a business where we had to provide service regardless of the elements or mechanical breakdown, and we weren't doing it. Our boats just couldn't take that kind of bad weather."

Miss Margy had been a definite step up, but she wasn't all that tough. One day, Bill was coming around the lighthouse in the *Margy* at cruising speed. Ahead was the *Algomah*, which made a hard, sharp turn, causing a short, sharp wake that Miss Margy had to cross. She crossed it and shuddered. Bill says, "I didn't think anything of it—but when we got to shore and I took a look, there were three breaks in the mainframe, by the chine (the place where the bottom meets the side)."

"Sometimes," Bill said, "we had to leave people on the island, and they'd have to stay over or take a different ferry back. It wasn't just the money we weren't making, although that certainly was important. We had an obligation to the customers, and we couldn't fulfill that obligation. It was very upsetting."

On windy, cold days in November, winds out of the northeast would create waves that would hit the dock and cause spray that would coat the trailer with ice. Chris remembers the trailer with affection and adds, "At least the trailer was frozen firmly in place."

The younger members of the family look back on those days as a happy time, even though dinner was often just eggs and pancakes, all they could afford. The boats and docks were their playground. By the time they were five or six, Chris and then Billy were helping passengers off and on the boats and showing them where to park.

Bill and his mother handled the bills. They'd spread them out on the floor and decide which ones they could afford to pay. Bill kept thinking that there had to be another way to make their business a success. One day, back from a charter, he was fueling *Miss Margy* when a solution suddenly hit him. They would have to become a ferry business rather than just chartering. He was amazed when, just a little later; his mother came to him with the same idea. "Dad and Mom and I were the board of directors," says Bill. "We would sit around the table, talk and plan, and then watch those plans become reality."

They figured that they could charge $3 a person. It was almost an instant success. They were carrying as many as sixteen people a trip and made $500 or $600 a day. In addition to her other duties, Marge sold tickets and answered the phone. Straits Transit cooperated with them—the men at Straits Transit were as eager to beat Arnold Transit as they were—and let the Shepler boats use their dock at Mackinac Island at no cost. Out of one conversation, the Shepler's ferry business was born.

As business increased in the early 1960s, Shepler's needed additional parking space. They purchased the former Windermere Hotel property from Don and Lucy Gridley in two separate transactions, the first in 1964 and the second in 1968. A short time later, Shepler's bought Harry Ryba's parking lot and dock that was located between the Gridley property and the Shepler dock. These transactions provided the Sheplers with a sizeable lot for accommodating their growing customer base along with a piece of prime waterfront real estate that was zoned for commercial use. Each step brought more business and served as vital collateral for expansion loans. According to Bill, "We were finding our way, slowly but surely, but with these transitions we were able to take a giant step forward."

Shepler's Topless

Frank Buchman, head of Moral Rearmament, was building a huge complex on Mackinac Island (later to become Mission Point Resort). He had a boat to take people to and from the island. She was called the *Kewadin* and was an all-weather boat that would go twenty-six miles per hour. When Bill crossed on her in twelve-to-thirteen-foot waves, he was amazed at the comfortable ride. This started Bill thinking. The need for a bigger, faster craft was apparent; it would allow them to operate in all kinds of weather.

Cap was also convinced that they had to grow if they were really going to prosper. In later years, Cap recalled, "We had to spend a lot of money. My son thought I was crazy, but I still had a little faith that with fast boats, we could trim the competition." That meant they had to have a really big boat with all-weather capability, seating for 120, and a top speed of thirty miles per hour. Bill says, "We didn't really know what we were getting into at the time. All we knew was that we didn't have the equipment to take care of the demand." They took a huge gamble. According to Marge's sister, Ellen, "They sold their property downstate and put everything in a boat." They also sold the speedboats, *Miss Penny* and *Fiji*.

Through a friend, Cap had met a marine architect from New Orleans and hired him. That was their first mistake. Mohammed Corcut told them that he could design an extra-special, fast, premium ferry boat. Too late, they found out that he really specialized in building barges. "He was blowing smoke," said Bill.

The vessel was built in the Great Lakes by T. D. Vinette, another mistake. The *Mein Kapitan* was made of steel, sixty feet long, powered by twin Cummings diesel engines—and a total disaster. For starters, it was supposed to be finished in July of 1967. Instead, it arrived in August, when the tourist season was almost over. Bill took one look at their dreamboat and saw that it was top-heavy and rode too high in the water. When it stopped at the fuel dock, it rocked in its own wake. However, the Coast Guard marine inspector, appropriately named CDR Drinkwater, passed it and signed the certificate.

Bill and Cap decided to make the best of it. Four or five days later, Cap was taking a full load of 120 passengers when he ran into a twenty-five-knot wind out of the east. As he was turning to come into the harbor, the vessel began to surf on a huge wave. To control and maintain direction of the vessel, Cap put one engine full speed ahead and the other in reverse; still, the boat continued to dangerously tip to one side. Cap, with one foot on the pilot house wall, was desperately trying to keep his balance when the boat finally righted itself. They made it to shore, the passengers disembarked, and Cap walked off. He handed the keys to Bill and said, "She's all yours!" Then he went home and poured himself a double Scotch.

Says Bill, "We realized that the boat was top-heavy; it needed more hull in the water to make it more stable, so I went out and bought eighty burlap sacks. In the dark of night, I filled each one with a hundred pounds of sand and stowed them in the stern compartment, which changed the trim."

It worked ... sort of. *Mein Kapitan*'s stability was improved, and she hadn't lost any speed. A few days later, Bill was taking on a full load of passengers on the island dock when a lieutenant from marine inspection came aboard and asked for Bill's license. Bill recalls, "It wasn't on the wall where it should have been. It was on my desk in Mackinaw City, and the lieutenant said, 'That's your first violation.' First violation? I knew we were in for it. Then the lieutenant said, 'Your trim has changed.' I said, 'We've just taken on a full load of fuel.' He said, 'Let's go look at your stern compartment,' and I knew we were dead. He ordered me to unload the sandbags and put it back to its original configuration.' I took the *Mein Kapitan* back to Mackinaw City. There I was with eight thousand pounds of sand that had to be hauled out of the stern and hoisted through a small hatch. What a job! Members of our staff helped. One person had to be down below to push the sandbags up through the hatch, and another was up top pulling them out. We finally got all the sand unloaded and dumped on the beach and then returned as fast as possible to Mackinac Island to pick up waiting passengers. As we were getting ready to depart the island with a full load of passengers, a Coast Guard seaman ran down the dock with a paper, yelling, 'You're not going anywhere. You're condemned!' He ordered me to return to Mackinaw City to meet with Commander Drinkwater. That was a really low point. We were publically condemned and humiliated in front of our passengers. And for a boat we had pinned all our hopes on—a boat that just wasn't working out.

"Commander Drinkwater demanded I take the *Mein Kapitan*'s certificate of inspection off the wall. It was the end of the season. We were broke and frustrated. I told him to take it off himself. He said, 'You can't run.' I told him I was going to call my attorney and sue him. He said, 'You don't want to do that.' I said, 'I certainly do. Look at that certificate. *You* signed it.' He thought it over and finally said, 'We'll recalculate and find out how to fix it on Monday.' It was Friday, and I couldn't afford to lose the weekend business. I said, 'We'll fix it this afternoon.' He finally agreed and started making his calculations. We still needed more weight below, so I called a foundry that made steel tubes and drums. The leftover hunks of metal are called slag. We got eight or nine thousand pounds of slag, washed it, and spray-painted it with red lead so it wouldn't rust. We had to weigh each piece and tag it with its weight. Drinkwater worked with me, making calculations while we put pieces of slag in the hull where he told us. He also insisted on taking the seats off the top deck so we would conform to stability regulations. All this work took about five days to complete. The final step in getting approval was a proof of stability test. The commander, by calculation, drew a line on the side of the hull and then placed fifty-five-gallon drums full of water. The drums, under his direction, were moved to the rail, causing the boat to 'heel.' The test was passed when the boat did not heel past the line that had been drawn on the hull. The test satisfied the commander. We got a new certificate, and for the rest of the season, we were able to use the *Mein Kapitan*.

"But I wasn't satisfied. Without the seats on the top deck, we could only carry eighty-five passengers instead of 120. The islanders nicknamed the boat *Shepler's Topless*. The engines weren't right, and the pitch of the propellers was too great, which overloaded the engines, causing unburnt fuel to go out the exhaust pipes in huge gusts of black, oily smoke. Because of the vibrations, the flex portion of the exhaust pipe cracked, allowing the oily exhaust to find its way out of the compartment through the vent pipe.

"During one crossing, three nuns were on the back deck, right by the vent pipe. At the end of the crossing, their white habits looked like speckled trout. I didn't know what to say to them, and they didn't say anything to me."

"We went for help to the premiere designer of fast yachts, J. B. Hargreave, whom Cap had known for many years. It turned out that the *Mein Kapitan* was top-heavy because Corcut had used the wrong weight factor for passengers; the average passenger weighed 165 pounds rather than the 145 pounds Corcut used. Hargreave designed modifications to get the stability and the propeller pitch right.

In the winter of 1966–67, the *Mein Kapitan* was in dry dock at the Christy Shipyard in Sturgeon Bay, Wisconsin. Their changes solved the stability issue and the other major problems, but *Mein Kapitan* was never really right. In spite of the design changes, she didn't have the speed they needed. David Armour says, "Shepler's built their reputation on speed. I always rode their line because they were faster—and the *Mein Kapitan* didn't have it."

The Sheplers finally sold the boat to Rodney Vorlock, of the Virgin Islands, and proceeded to sue both the original designer and the shipyard that had built her. William Crane had been Cap's lawyer for years. When he retired in the 1960s, his son William took over and handled Shepler's legal work. He says, "I sat in on a lot of meetings with the Sheplers and their CPA. It was interesting to see how an up-and-coming business plans for the future." Crane says he got a real education preparing the *Mein Kapitan* case: he had to study boat construction and Coast Guard inspections. The suit established case law nationwide because the boat builder was in Michigan and the naval architect was in Louisiana. William Crane had to defend Shepler's right to bring the naval architect to Michigan and sue him in Michigan courts. According to Crane, "We won this nationwide, precedent-setting decision that confirmed Michigan's 'long arm statute' over nonresidents who cause damage in Michigan."

Despite *Mein Kapitan's* problems, Shepler's was still the fastest ferry line. Bill says, "It was another step in our growth."

Dreamboats

Having learned plenty of lessons from the *Mein Kapitan* fiasco, in the late sixties, Shepler's once again tried for a dreamboat. They went to J. B. Hargreave and told him what they needed in a ferry: speed, comfort, appearance, and seaworthiness. Hargreave designed a boat that incorporated all their ideas.

To find a boatyard to build the new ferry, Shepler's turned to Louisiana's bayou country where Cajun boatyards build vessels to carry crews to offshore oil rigs in the Gulf of Mexico. Says Bill, "Dad, the designer, the salesman from the engine builder, and I got together in Louisiana and visited several shipyards. We decided on the Cam Craft Yard of Crown Point, Louisiana; it was a boatyard with thirty years' experience."

But there was a problem. Bill Shepler took the plans to their bank in Saginaw, Michigan. He needed money to build the boat, but the bank would only loan the money if Shepler's could guarantee that the vessel would go thirty miles per hour and have the stability to carry 120 passengers. It was a classic Catch-22 situation.

Hargreave wouldn't guarantee the boat would go thirty mph because he wasn't going to build it. The boatyard wouldn't guarantee it because they didn't design it. The Sheplers were stymied.

But then the president of Saginaw's Michigan National Bank joined one of the ski trips Bill organized. Bill taught him to ski, and on the plane ride back, he expressed his gratitude and said, "Now what can I do for you?"

Bill said, "You can loan me $75,000 to build a boat." There was still a problem: the bank needed verification of speed and capacity. This problem was ultimately solved when they discovered that Cam Craft had already built a sixty-five-foot crew boat of similar design that would go thirty-two miles per hour and was almost identical in horsepower to the prospective ferry. Michigan National okayed the loan.

The workers in the boatyard called the new ferry *Proud Mary,* but Shepler's wanted a name based on Great Lakes history. They consulted Mackinac State Historic Parks deputy director and history researcher, David Armour. He suggested the name *Welcome,* for a sloop that had aided in the evacuation of the original Fort Michilimackinac from Mackinaw City to the island. The original *Welcome* carried supplies and timber from

the mainland and brought up soldiers from Detroit. She was considered a very fast sailing sloop in her time.

The new *Welcome* was described as a new concept of high speed and modern transportation, not only in the Straits area but in the entire Great Lakes region. Bill's friend Dick Babcock said, "Bill brought the idea of fast boats to the Straits when they introduced large boats with planing hulls. He built lightweight aluminum hulls that went fast. Bill also standardized all engines and marine gears so his mechanics could swap them out and get boats running quickly."

Dick is in the boatyard business and considers all northern Michigan marinas as partners, not competitors. He adds, "Bill is very fussy about the way boats are kept and operations run. He has clean, disciplined, friendly crews that look good and work fast. Even the competitors take their boats to Shepler's if they need repairs."

In July 1969, Cam Craft called to say that the *Welcome* was finished. She was a sixty-foot twin diesel vessel with V-drives and a top speed of thirty mph. She offered her 120 passengers a stable, comfortable ride in all kinds of weather.

Cap went down to pick her up. He called home all excited and told Bill, "It's a Goddamn speedboat!"

As Cap was traveling up the Mississippi on his way home to Mackinaw City, a tornado struck. Cap hung on for dear life, fighting to control the boat, as the wind swirled the boat helplessly around in the river, going aground and bending the propellers. Once the tornado passed, Cap was able to navigate the wounded boat to the dock. He called the Cam Craft manager, Tony Bergeron, and Cam Craft came to the rescue. Bergeron flew on an amphibious airplane to where Cap was docked, bringing with him a spare set of propellers. He got the propellers changed and stayed with Cap and the boat for the rest of the trip.

Everyone was waiting on shore for the *Welcome*'s arrival. Years later, Cap recalled the triumph he felt when they came under the bridge at full speed. Even a competitor was out on his dock when the *Welcome* arrived. Cap remembered, "When that *Welcome* came around the point, I blew the whistle and flew the flag so he could see her. I came around the end of the dock, and she was going like mad. I landed that *Welcome* up front where everyone could see her!"

Cap's interviewer from the *Petoskey News Review* added, "If that competitor suspected his days were numbered, it was confirmed a few years later when Shepler's bought him out."

That competitor was Harry Ryba, who started Lakeview Transit in the summer of 1968. Harry was an entrepreneur who already had a very successful fudge company and had obtained licenses to rent out four hundred bicycles, another profitable venture. Bill says, "One day, he came over and started asking Cap about the ferry business. Cap was always ready for a chat, and Harry really picked his brains. Cap told him everything. A little later, Ryba was able to purchase property right next to Shepler's dock, and soon thereafter, he started Lake View Transit right next to our dock."

Shepler's and Ryba's Lake View Transit engaged in spirited, free enterprise competition. Each had workers waving potential passengers onto its dock. Shepler's had a slight advantage because it was located on the eastbound lane of Main Street, so potential passengers drove right onto its property on Main Street. To get to the Lake View Transit Dock, people had to cross over to westbound Main Street.

Shepler's had another advantage: its vessels were superior. Ryba's vessels were one-level, enclosed launch boats that were slower than the Shepler vessels, yet faster than the Arnold Transit and Star Line boats.

Shepler's, on the other hand, had the two-level, faster, 120- passenger *Welcome*. In addition, the Sheplers had ordered a new 150-passenger vessel named *Felicity*.

Early in 1972, Shepler's found a buyer for the *Mein Kapitan* and negotiated the sale contingent upon the arrival of the *Felicity*. Seeing the writing on the wall, Harry decided to stick with fudge and bikes rather than try to build a ferry line. He sold out to Shepler's.

Lake View Transit had two sixty-two-foot steel planing boats, the *Patricia R.* and the *Ethyl Marie*. Each carried eighty-five passengers. Shepler's wanted to sell both boats, which were nowhere near as sleek and fast as the *Welcome*, but they needed all the capacity they could get, due to the growth of the company. Shepler's managed to sell the *Patricia R.* but chose to continue to use the *Ethyl Marie* for four more years before selling it to a firm in South America.

Shepler's had moved from facing possible failure with the *Mein Kapitan* to building the *Welcome* and the *Felicity* and purchasing two other boats from Lakeview Transit. This was sufficient capacity to handle their growth spurt in the early seventies.

Shepler's market share in the highly competitive Mackinac Straits ferry boat competition grew substantially in 1972. The *Welcome* got even faster. Bill says, "We put in bigger injectors; she was the fastest boat on the Great Lakes at the time, reaching speeds of up to thirty-six miles per hour. I drove her, and we called her the Silver Bullet. Dad didn't know how fast she was. The first time he drove her after the injector change, he floored her when they got into open water. She lurched forward, throwing Dad out of the pilot house and into the second row of seats on the top deck. He yelled, '*What* have you done to my boat?'"

By this time, Bill's youngsters, who had grown up on the docks, were taking a more active role in the business. When she was in the ninth grade, Kathy started assisting her grandmother in the ticket office. By the early seventies, Chris was handling the bow line on the *Welcome*. He says with a grin, "Once when Dad was docking the *Welcome* at the dock on the island, he was talking to someone and bumped into the dock. I fell into the water, and they had to pull me out."

The experience didn't stop Chris. Cap taught him how to drive the boats. Chris says, "He was the last of the old school in terms of navigation. I'm a captain because of him."

Before the *Welcome*, luggage was carried aboard the boats by hand and stacked on the aft deck. It was a slow and cumbersome process, and luggage was sometimes lost or damaged. Bill decided to match the speed and style of the new boat with a completely new, speedy way to handle luggage: a four-by-six-foot cart with pneumatic tires that would hold up to sixty bags at one time. Their idea for the luggage carts was so innovative that there were none on the market. He took his drawings to three aluminum fabricating shops, and they all told him it couldn't be done. ("Don't tell him something can't be done," Chris says of his dad.) Shepler's own aluminum welder, Steve Socolovitch, said it could be done, and he did it.

Bill worked out the best method of loading the carts. Large and heavy bags are placed on first. Small, medium, and lightweight bags make up the second tier. Golf bags go on next with each bag reversed; garment bags go on last. They are all secured with shrink wrap and covered with a canvas if it's raining. The system makes it easy to put all the luggage for one hotel on a single cart for fast, efficient delivery.

The carts have been popular—maybe a little too popular. They were widely copied, and people started leaving them all over the island. The island government was upset. First they started impounding carts, and then they passed a cart-zoning law. Bill explains how the law was written. "It said we couldn't push a cart off our dock to a hotel or business unless it was a three-by-six personal cart. Otherwise, the cart had to be attached to a horse-drawn dray."

Over the years, improvements have been incorporated into various types of personal transportation. The same is true of each new ferry. The

Hope was built in 1975 to carry 150 passengers. Billy Shepler says of her, "The *Hope* is so sturdy that you could drop her from a hundred feet onto concrete and her hull would be okay."

More ferries were needed, and in 1979, the *Wyandot* joined the fleet. The *Wyandot* was a seventy-seven-foot boat, and J. B. Hargreave had designed her with three engines instead of two. The back of the boat was flat so that the middle screw was at the same depth as the other two. At David Armour's suggestion, the *Felicity,* the *Hope,* and the *Wyandot* were also named for famous

British vessels that sailed the Straits area at the time of the Revolutionary War. Also, Wyandotte was the name of the downriver Detroit area where the Sheplers lived for many years.

The choppy waves of the Straits demand sturdy boats, they have to withstand the sudden impact when a big wave lifts the vessel and drops it. "Bogus waves" occasionally pose a problem. The waves will be running from eight to ten feet when suddenly, a twenty-foot wall of water appears out of nowhere. That's what happened some years later when the *Wyandot* was going from Mackinaw City to the island. She rose up twenty feet and then dropped like a stone. Some passengers were thrown from their seats, but no one was hurt.

With a larger fleet and an ever-increasing number of passengers, it became obvious that the Mackinac Island dock was no longer adequate. In the fall of 1981, Shepler's built a covered waiting area with a large, barrier-free restroom area and seventy-two lockers where personal items could be safely stored. The expansion tripled Shepler's usable space on the island. In 1985, they were finally able to expand their operation in St. Ignace by buying a large tract of land on the north side of the city. A master plan was developed for the area with large parking lots, underground utilities, a dredged harbor, and modern restrooms. There were also floating docks that offered boat slips to attract twelve yachts. The St. Ignace dock also became home to Shepler's Freight Service (see "Delivering the Goods").

In 1987, the main entrance to the Mackinaw City Dock was developed into a gateway with flags and landscaping. The intention was to signify The Gateway to Mackinac Island.

Rose LaPointe came to work for Shepler's in the eighties. She thought it was a one-day job when her Aunty Marge asked her to fill in at the ticket office for the afternoon, but she's been selling tickets ever since. Rose remembers their first office. "There was hardly enough room for two people, and sometimes we had as many as five: two out in front, one on each side, and when we got really busy, we'd open the back door and someone would sell tickets there."

How was she trained for the job? "My Aunty Marge said, 'Okay—here's the chair, and here are all the tickets.' That was all the training we got. Marge was head ticket seller, and she didn't need an adding machine; she had all the figures in her head. At the end of the day, we had to check out, and we couldn't go home until we got it right. Marge was strong-willed, and she knew what was right and wrong. When she told you to do something, you did it—no fooling around."

Cap could be equally exacting when it came to boat safety. When Rose was a little girl, she was waiting on the dock for the *Miss Penny*. When the speedboat came in, she jumped aboard without waiting for Cap to tie up. He gave her a stern lecture, ending with, "Don't you *ever* do that again!"

Otherwise, Cap was his usual genial self. Sue LaCross in accounting says, "Every once in a while, someone would show up at the ticket office with a card or even a paper napkin that said, 'This person has free passage for life—signed, Cap.' Of course, we always honored it."

Bill adds, "A maitre d' at the Grand Hotel has been crossing on one of the Cap's cards for thirty years."

Flowers on the Water

Cap and Marge traveled extensively during the off season and spent time at Briny Breeze in Florida, just south of Palm Beach. It was a friendly trailer park which offered a community hall and many activities. Cap and Marge had bought their trailer site back in the 1950s, when that kind of Florida real estate was very inexpensive. Marge cleaned houses in the more affluent areas nearby. Their lot and dock faced on the inland waterway, so they were always near the water. Later on, Bill and his family joined them in Florida for several weeks each year. Patty, Bill's daughter and the Shepler's office manager, recalls fishing with her grandfather, listening to his stories, and watching Cap and Marge square dance.

The last of the Shepler's ferries was named in honor of Cap. It was 1986 and he was in poor health, but he was excited about going to Louisiana to get his namesake. Bill and Billy went with him, and Billy remembers the trip vividly: "It was a great trip. We went through seventeen locks on the Mississippi. I grew up on the Straits, and the scenery was different. So was the experience of running on a river: there were lots of currents but no waves like on the Straits. Sometimes we had to climb up over forty-foot-high levies to reach

the towns after we tied up for the evening. And the trip was very special to me because it was a chance to get to know my granddad better."

The Mississippi is a challenge to navigate because the river is constantly changing. Bill recalls, "One morning, Dad wanted to drive. The river widened, and we started right down the middle. Fortunately, I looked at the chart and found that the course actually went a half mile to the left. We had to backtrack, following our own wake, and start over. Had we continued on the way were going, we would have gone aground for sure."

There were bridges along their route that hadn't been opened in thirty years. To get under them, they had to dismantle the radar and take down the spar and anything higher than the pilot house. When that still wasn't enough, they lowered the whole boat by flooding the first and second compartments, thus lowering the bow and raising the stern. The lock at Lockport, Illinois, had sixty-foot doors. As they approached, the lockmaster told them to get over to the side and secure all lines because a barge and its tug were waiting on the other side to get through. When the lockmaster opened the slues, tons of water rushed through. They stayed there all through a long, rough night.

But something far rougher happened on one of their last nights as they were going through the Illinois Drainage Canal. It was something that changed Bill and Cap's lives and their relationship. Bill remembers it vividly. "Cap was driving the *Capt. Shepler* that night. The boat had four identical buttons on the dash: three for the engines and one for the horn. The buttons weren't marked, so we had to remember which was which. That night, the engines were three-quarters open, going at 1,500 rpm. You never push a starter button on an engine going that fast. The teeth would be chewed off the starter crank, and it would never start the engine again. I was helping Cap when suddenly I noticed his hand come up to sound the horn to warn a tug ahead of us. But his hand was going to the wrong button. At the last minute, I pushed his hand away."

Bill recalls the rest of the story with pain in his voice after more than twenty years. "Dad looked at me and walked away. I said, 'Dad, I'm sorry.' He said, 'You embarrassed me in front of my friends.' And I thought, 'I can't tell this man who's one of the greatest captains on the Great Lakes how to drive a boat.' I don't know if it was age, disability, or his diabetes. I wondered about his capability. He had such pride: he was a great navigator, a great boatman, and a great captain."

Years later, Bill told an interviewer, "I never said to Cap, 'It's time for you to leave.' That would have killed him, just as it would kill me if my kids were to say that to me."

Cap never completely retired and remained Bill's most loved and respected consultant until he died in 1988, two years after their trip up the Mississippi. Cap had never been a solemn person, and the whole family knew that a solemn funeral wouldn't suit him. As the one who knew him the best, Marge planned the service from start to finish.

It was a cold, gray day, the kind old-timers would have called a "fisherman's day." Friends and admirers came from all over northern Michigan and from Detroit and Grand Rapids to pay their respects. There was standing room only in Mackinaw City's Church of the Straits, a simple frame building that was bright with flowers that day. Bill read Cap's favorite poem, "The Wreck of the Wood Skow *Julie Plaunt*." Cap had always delighted in delivering it with a strong French-Canadian accent:

> T'was one dark night on Lac St Clair, da wind she blow blow blow
> And da crew on da wood scow Julie Plaunt got scare and go below.
> Da Capt. she walk on da front deck, she walk on da hind deck too
> She call da crew from up da hole, she call da cook also
> Da cook she's name Rosie, she come from Montreal
> She was a chambermaid on a lumber barge on the ol' Lachine Canal
> Da Capt. she's trow da hank, but still dot scow she drift
> Da cannot pass on that shore for fear da loose dat skiff
> Da wind she blow from N.E.W. da south wind too
> And Rosie say 'Oh Capt., whatever shall I do?'
> Da wind she blows like hurricane, and by and by she blow some more
> Da cow buss up right off Gross Point, ten acres from da shore
> Da nite she dark like ten black cat, da wave she run high and fass

Da Capt. take poor Rosie and lash her to da mast
Da Capt. put on the life preserver and jumps into da Lac
And he say 'Goodbye my Rosie dear, I go down for your sac'
Da next morn very herly, half past 1,2,3,4 da Capt. cook and wood scow
Lay corpses on that shore
Now all my good scow sailor men, take lesson from dat storm
And you never get drown on Lac St Clair so long you stay on da shore.

As he finished the reading, Bill added, "I hope that St. Peter understands French when Cap gets to the gate."

After the service, some three hundred mourners were taken to the Shepler dock, where they boarded the *Hope,* the *Wyandot,* and the *Capt. Shepler.* As they came on board, each was handed a red rose. The family was on *Capt. Shepler* along with the Mackinaw City High School marching band, which played some of Cap's best-loved tunes, such as "Anchors Aweigh."

As they pulled out into the Straits, they were surprised to be joined by fifteen other vessels, including two Arnold Line ferries, two from the Star Line, and a group of privately owned yachts. They all fell in line behind the Shepler's boats.

Bill had equipped the *Capt. Shepler* with a device they had invented for a "man overboard" rescue. A ladder, attached by hooks to the boat's ramp, went down to a hinged platform about a foot above the water. Bill climbed down, and as the band played "Amazing Grace," he spread Cap's ashes on the waves. A patch of blue sky suddenly broke through the clouds, and a single ray of sunshine shone on the scene. The *Capt. Shepler* sounded the Great Lake's Salute (one long, two short). This salute was echoed, one at a time, by each of the other boats as passengers dropped their roses into the water.

Bill says, "Looking back, I could see just where Cap was resting by the flowers on the water." It was a heartfelt tribute to a great man -- a great captain.

This was a most difficult moment for Bill. Cap was gone. Bill couldn't quite grasp this loss of his father, his friend, and his mentor. Bill had so much respect for the great captain, who was a great husband, great father, and great friend to the many people who had delighted in his warmth and humor as they rode with him on the many vessels he had captained. His legacy would last forever. His son Bill was now in charge. He knew what he had to do, and his dad had prepared him well. The second generation of Shepler's Mackinac Island Ferry was launched.

Delivering the Goods

Shepler's not only runs ferries from St. Ignace to the island but is also a freight business. Back in 1993, Chris presented an idea to the rest of the family. "The Mission Point Resort and Conference Center had talked to me about it, and we figured that other places in the area could also use the service. The whole family was at Mom and Dad's; I had flip charts and the business plan to show them how it would work. I heard about a sixty-five-foot boat for sale that had been a car ferry running from Sandusky, Ohio, to Put-In-Bay and Catawba Island. Dad, Billy, and I flew down to Sandusky to look her over and take a ride. We flew back and decided to buy her. Billy and I drove down in the Suburban, put the car on board, and brought the boat back. We ran into a storm on Saginaw Bay and almost lost the car, but we finally made it home." Chris explained the naming of the vessel when he said, "We named her the *Sacre Bleu,* which was Granddad's favorite expression. We ran freight that fall and the next summer and did okay, but we realized that the big money was in running heavy equipment to the island. We hired Tim Graul, a naval architect out of Sturgeon Bay, to design a thirty-foot extension to the midsection, making the *Sacre Bleu* ninety-five feet long, just big enough to carry a large propane truck.

Now we had to get her to Basic Marine in Escanaba to get the work done. It was the middle of December with ice everywhere and the temperature at twenty-five degrees when Billy and I headed out. We were able to tuck behind a freighter for a while, but it was a miserable twenty-four hours. By the time we reached Green Bay, the temperature had dropped to twenty degrees below zero. We didn't have much to eat, nor did we have proper heating aboard. This coupled with the fact that Billy was suffering with the flu made this a trip from hell. But, like always, we got it done. Green Bay looked like a big frozen margarita, and the *Sacre Bleu* got stuck in the ice. Finally, a tug came along and made circles around us to break the ice, and we got loose and into Escanaba. Billy was coaching the Harbor Springs High School ski team at the time, and he had to meet them. I stayed on board to move the boat to dry dock. What a night! I had to sleep on the cold steel deck and almost froze. Then at nine thirty that night, I got a phone call from Kathy. Dad had been in a head-on collision five miles south of Mackinaw City. The other car had crossed the yellow line on a hill and crashed into him. We flew back and found that Dad was okay but pretty beat up, with several broken ribs."

The boat got finished and was certified by the Coast Guard to go anywhere in the Great Lakes. The stretch made the *Sacre Bleu* more stable, and she could carry loads up to 150 tons. The wiring and piping also had to be modified. She's powered by twin-screw Detroit Diesel engines and draws eight feet unloaded and nine feet with a 200,000-pound load. There were many times that contractors with heavy equipment could not cross the bridge because of excessive weight. These contractors would hire Shepler's to transport their heavy equipment across the Straits, to and from Cheboygan.

Shepler's freight manager, Chris Menominee, and his crew of eight unload trucks and load the *Sacre Bleu,* using forklifts, electric tugs, and muscle. Chris inventories shipments and arrivals and is in charge of invoicing. The freight office is open six days a week, from five a.m. to five p.m. Monday through Friday and five a.m. to noon on Saturdays. They deliver from April through January, "or whatever Mother Nature determines."

The *Sacre Bleu* makes one to two trips to Mackinac Island every day, carrying everything from Special K cereal to construction materials. Almost everyone on the island relies on her deliveries: bed and breakfasts, hotels, and restaurants get food supplies almost every day. The *Sacre Bleu* also carries FedEx deliveries, since they don't run their own vessels to service the Island. She carries all kinds of heavy equipment: bulldozers, dump trucks for paving, golf carts, etc. Once at Mackinac Island, cargo is picked up and delivered by bicycles or horse-drawn drays. The freight boat, on demand, carries large-load equipment from St. Ignace to Cheboygan when it's too big or too heavy to cross on the bridge, which has a maximum of 172,000 pounds.

An unexpected use for the boat is as a cruise ship for parties and receptions. She's wide and comfortable, can carry up to 150 or more guests, can be dressed up for special occasions with appropriate decorations, and she has a liquor license. (The ferries can also be dressed up for parties: the seats in the cabin are taken out, and a buffet and drinks can be served there.)

The freight business has had some tough times. Politics can be a problem. When Shepler's first applied for a freight license, the island government didn't want to give it to them, citing narrow streets and congestion. When they finally did get a license, they found that Arnold Transit was allowed to operate twenty-four hours a day while Shepler's could only unload from six a.m. to nine a.m. Then, in 2004, the island government tried to take away their license completely. When customers called to cancel, Shepler's attorney went to work and threatened a lawsuit based on the fact that the island was giving preferential treatment to Arnold's under the guise of regulation. The license was finally renewed with hours extended to ten thirty a.m., which Chris describes as "better than nothing." He says. "The people on Mackinac Island want us; we offer better service at lower prices. So we keep plugging away."

Some jobs can be challenging. Chris tells about the time they transported a giant air filter from a stone quarry in the UP to Charlevoix. "The thing was twenty-five feet by twenty-five feet and looked like a giant milk jug. We chained it down, but it was so big and stuck up so high it was hard to control. Going into Charlevoix, I was afraid that we were going to lose it. Another time, we had a contract with a local paving company to carry semis full of hot liquid tar to make asphalt for a paving project on Beaver Island. The trip took sixteen hours, from three p.m. to six a.m., and we made twenty-five trips. The Coast Guard would have had our heads if those semis full of eight-hundred-degree tar had gone into Lake Michigan. When we got back to St. Ignace the last time, we kissed the ground."

Another unusual—but not so difficult—cargo was a life-sized plastic elephant named Victory that went to the island for the Bi-Annual Michigan Republican Convention. The elephant was originally sculpted by Midland artist Ted Abbey and had been the star of the 1984 Republican National Convention. The Budweiser Clydesdales have travelled on the *Sacre Bleu* in their own immaculate semis.

In 2007, the same year that the Mackinac Bridge celebrated its fiftieth anniversary, the CBS *Early Show* was on tour visiting the coolest islands in America, which of course included Mackinac Island. The sponsor of CBS's summer program was the RV builder Winnebago. One of their RVs was shown on national TV, crossing the straits on the deck of the *Sacre Bleu*.

And in 2012, the Sheplers hosted the Harlem Globetrotters on the Sacre Bleu for their trip to the island for an exhibition game. On the way over, they performed for an audience of 150 guests in one of the most memorable rides to Mackinac Island that Shepler's had ever experienced.

In July of 2011, Shepler's decided it was time to upgrade the *Sacre Bleu*. Built in 1954, the *Bleu* still met Coast Guard standards. Said Fleet Captain Billy Shepler, "We could have run her for five more years in the original condition, but we wanted her to be the best." They hired a naval architect to draw up plans and then waited for government approval for eight months. Billy remarked, "It took twice as long to get the government OK as it did to make the changes." It was estimated that the job would take six to nine months. It was finished in four. Moran Iron Works of Onaway did the job. They took twenty-five feet off the bow and replaced it with a new bow section designed especially for the pressures of weather, ice, and wave conditions in the Straits area. The new bow was built to match the boat. The high girders and plates forming the new bow added forty tons of steel to the vessel. She needed icebreaking capability. "We wanted a boat that could work in the harshest of weather- the worst of the worst a northern Michigan winter can dish out. We needed it to break ice so we could do our best to serve the island and its residents. We're not even sure of her limitations yet, because we haven't seen the most she can do. She just keeps surprising us." stated Bill Shepler. The *Bleu* was outfitted with two new MTU Series 60 engines. These four cycle engines add five-hundred more horsepower to the boat. They are not only state of the art and very powerful, but they are also clean and efficient. The original cabin and pilot house were removed. They had held only twenty-two passengers. Their heated replacements carry fifty-five passengers in comfort during the early spring and late fall periods when weather conditions prevent the Shepler ferries from running. In addition, new electric and electronic systems were installed. The whole project cost 2.2 million dollars. Said Billy, "There are few, if any, boats on the Great Lakes that have the *Bleu*'s performance capacity. The winter of 2014 proved that our huge investment really made sense. The rebuilt *Sacre Bleu* is so much more than we thought!"

As a result, more and more Straits businesses have selected Shepler's to deliver their freight. They include the Grand Hotel, the Island's most important business, Mission Point Resort, and the Windermere Hotel and Doud's Grocery Store, both owned by the family of Mayor Margaret Doud.

Shepler's was also chosen to transport the Island's six-hundred-and-fifty huge draft horses from their winter quarters in the Upper Peninsula. *Sacre Bleu* is able to carry up to twenty-four horses in their trailers on a single trip. With no motorized vehicles allowed on the Island, the horses are absolutely essential to the economy, moving all the freight and providing carriage service.

One major problem remained. Both Shepler's and the Islanders had been concerned about the congestion and delays caused by unloading freight at the Shepler dock in downtown Mackinac Island where thousands of tourists were coming and going. Shepler's and Mission Point Resort suggested that the Beaver dock at Mission Point would be a far better alternative. Mission Point Resort leased the Beaver dock back to the city of Mackinac Island which, in turn, leased it to Shepler's for 60 days. It looked like an ideal solution but one Beaver dock neighbor strongly objected and sought a temporary restraining order. The local judge granted his request. After stopping Shepler's from operating over the Memorial Day weekend, the judge finally recused himself. A new judge was appointed the Tuesday after Memorial Day and quickly dismissed the restraining order, allowing the City of Mackinac Island the use of the Beaver Dock for freight, thus allowing any freight company the use of that dock.

The winter of 2013-14 was bitterly cold with more ice covering the Lakes than in any year since 1979. According to meteorologists, they were 92.19% frozen over. Usually, the ice lasts from approximately January 15 to April 15 and the shipping season is able to get started in late March or early April. In 2014, as late as April 26, freighters were lined up in the St. Mary's River, waiting to go through the one Soo Lock that was open. Chris Shepler said, "I have never seen it like this, and I am 52 years old."

Mackinac Island was especially hard hit. With no shipping, they had to rely on the supplies that could be flown in on small planes or snowmobiles that could cross on an ice bridge between the Island and St. Ignace. It was a tough time for the hardy souls who wintered on the Island and someone described their plight as "being trapped in an ice prison." Spring came late and many seasonal businesses were forced to delay their usual opening dates. The Grand Hotel had to cancel the first weekend of their 128th anniversary celebration. One bright note was that the unusual weather conditions gave the new *Bleu* a chance to show what she could do.

First, they had to wait for the Coast Guard to make a couple of passes between the Island and St. Ignace. The thick ice bridge was still in place after 120 days. The record for the bridge lasting was 80 days and some years, it was gone in 30 days. On April

22, a Coast Guard icebreaker was able to break through the three feet of ice. After the breakthrough, the ice blew out and separated from the beach. The ice bridge was gone. However, the icebreaker couldn't get close to the Island since it was too big for the shallow harbor. That's when the *Bleu* went to work. Said Billy, "On Wednesday, April 23, we started breaking out from St. Ignace. We got the *Bleu* turned around facing the Island and we spent six hours, cutting through a mile and a half of two feet of blue ice. No problem! We went back to our dock and the next day, we took a load of freight to the Island. It took us half an hour to get through half a mile of ice to the harbor. A crowd of people were out on our dock cheering and waving. As soon as we cleared the lighthouse, I leaned on the horn, blowing the master salute, three long blasts and two short. What a thrill! I was so proud and happy-- and I thought of my Grandpa Cap and the day he brought the Welcome up to Mackinaw City, blowing the horn in the master salute to the cheering crowds on shore."

Great Lakes Lighthouse Keepers Association

The Great Lakes Lighthouse Keepers Association (GLLKA) was started in 1982 by members of lighthouse keepers' families who started meeting to simply share stories. Others who were interested in lighthouses began to join these family gatherings. Dick Moehl was one of those people. Dick put wheels on their wagon, so to speak, when he organized the group into a 501(c)(3) business structure. He served as its president and as a board member for nearly three decades. Dick resigned from GLLKA in December 2012. According to today's executive director, Terry Pepper, "GLLKA was built into what it is today by Dick's passionate commitment to keeping the lighthouse legacy alive."

GLLKA's survival and growth is due in large part to collaboration with the Shepler's Mackinac Island Ferry business. Dick shared the story of how he stopped in Cheboygan to buy some lighthouse pictures. While discussing the photos, Dick was struck with a new idea: perhaps he should buy a boat and take his own pictures. That idea morphed into a bigger idea in Dick's mind. He thought, "What if we took people with us on cruises where they could see the lighthouses up close and take their own pictures while being educated about the history and significance of each lighthouse?"

Dick first took his idea to Arnold Line, but he was quickly informed that since the tours would go beyond the official boundaries of the Straits area, the captain would need to possess an unlimited license—and Cap Shepler was the only ferry boat captain with that credential. Based on that information, Dick proposed his idea to Cap Shepler. According to Dick, "Cap initially thought that the idea was crazy, but he changed his mind when the first lighthouse tour turned out to be an overwhelming success." Based on this success, Dick asked Cap to design two three-hour cruises, one that would go east and the other west, and cost them out so as to benefit GLLKA. The lighthouse tours were born, and this collaboration became the first maritime fundraising effort in the area.

A couple of years later, when Cap died, Bill Shepler expanded the tours to include extended cruises to other areas and, most recently, nighttime cruises. Today, Bill Shepler and all of Shepler's Captains are licensed to conduct these tours. According to Fleet Captain Billy Shepler, all of our captains can take boats into any area of the straits. The limitations they face today have to do with the boats themselves, i.e. stability, tonnage capacity and things of that sort that are monitored by the Coast Guard".

By 2002, Shepler's was conducting up to forty-two lighthouse cruises per season, with GLLKA experts narrating. According to Dick Moehl, these cruises generate about a half-million dollars in revenue for the Straits area per year. Many people who come for a Tuesday eastbound tour stick around for the Thursday westbound tour. These tourists also spend money on hotel rooms, restaurants, carriage rides, bicycle rentals, and memorabilia.

I joined the Shepler crew and a boatload of passengers (wearing my "Captain Don" cap) to enjoy the eastbound lighthouse tour. I was surprised to witness Captain Bill enter from the back of the boat while doing a spot-on imitation of Foster Brooks, acting as if he were beyond intoxicated. I could see the emotions of the passengers change from initial shock to hearty laughter as they saw that he was pulling their legs. Upon exiting the ferry, one passenger asked Captain Bill, "Have you sobered up yet?"

As we pulled away from the dock Terry Pepper began to educate the passengers about how and why each lighthouse was built, describe the significance of lighthouses to safe navigation in the Straits, and tell humorous stories involving the lighthouses and their caretakers.

Terry informed me that he got interested in lighthouses in 1988. He began to take pictures of land-based lighthouses and hitched rides to observe and take pictures of those that could only be reached by water. Being an Internet junkie, he tried to learn all he could about lighthouses. He focused mostly on the western Great Lakes: Lake Huron, Lake Michigan, and Lake Superior. His quest to share what he had learned was enhanced when he created a website entitled "Seeing the Light" in 1995. The site became a magnet for people interested in lighthouses, and Terry was frequently invited to join people on different lighthouse tours. For example, Bob Mackreth, parks historian with Apostle's Islands National Lake Shore Park, asked Terry to join him on their annual lighthouse inspection tour.

Terry was becoming well known, and his expertise was rewarded when the GLLKA board of directors hired him as executive director of GLLKA in 2006. From the outset, one of his responsibilities was narrating the lighthouse cruises, a task that Dick Moehl and Sandy Planisek had handled for years. He shared the narrating responsibilities with Dick and Sandy until Sandy resigned.

In my eastbound tour, I also learned that the lighthouses were built to help mariners navigate safely around the Great Lakes. The lakes were the highways, and the lighthouses guided their travel. I learned that each lighthouse has its own unique characteristics, such as flashing lights, stable lights, and colored lights—and that no two lighthouses in a given area have the same characteristics. I was amazed when Terry informed the passengers that the offshore lighthouses were constructed by first building an eighty- or ninety-foot-square box, filling it with rocks and cement, and then building the lighthouse structure on top of the sunken box.

I enjoyed my eastbound lighthouse cruise so much that I plan to take the westbound cruise next season. Of particular interest to me was Terry's explanation of how the range lights serve to guide vessels safely into the mouth of the Cheboygan River. There are two lights, 1,500 feet apart. When the taller rear light is lined up directly above the shorter, front light, a vessel is directed straight up the center of the narrow channel into the river.

The Eastbound Lighthouse Cruise includes the following: Old Mackinac Point Lighthouse, Round Island Lighthouse, Round Island Passage Light, Bois Blanc Island Lighthouse, Poe Reef Light, Fourteen Foot Shoal Light, and Cheboygan Range Lights. The extended eastbound cruise adds Spectacle Reef Light between Bois Blanc and Poe Reef. The westbound cruise includes the following: Old Mackinac Point Lighthouse, St. Helena Island Lighthouse, White Shoal Light, Grays Reef Light, and Waugoshance Lighthouse. The extended westbound Cruise adds Ile Aux Galets, or Skillagalee to locals, between Grays Reef and Waugoshance.

The Les Cheneaux Cruise is a third option for lighthouse tourists. This cruise includes the following: a scenic cruise among Les Cheneaux Islands, Martin Reef Light, Detour Reef Light, Spectacle Reef Light, Bois Blanc Island Lighthouse, Round Island Passage Light, and Round Island Lighthouse.

Cindy Gezon, Shepler's groups and cruises coordinator, filled me in about night cruises. "Emmet County received an International Dark Sky Park designation for the Headlands property in May 2011. It is one of just a small number of recognized Dark Sky Parks in the United States, so when Shepler's was approached by Mary Stewart Adams, the Dark Sky Park program director at the Headlands, about offering evening cruises that would appeal to visitors and local residents alike, we were eager to develop a new public cruise product to add to our schedule".

For the 2012 season, Shepler's put together four moon cruises—a new moon cruise in June, a full moon cruise in July, a blue moon cruise in August, and a harvest moon cruise in September. Each cruise took guests out under the Mackinac Bridge and out toward the Headlands shoreline to watch the sunset and moonrise, with narration provided by Mary Stewart Adams. Her narration includes sky lore, information about how indigenous peoples viewed the constellations, and a description of the role of the stars in ancient cultures. She also includes poetry and music that follow a celestial theme in her presentations.

According to Mary Stewart Adams, "My goal is to raise awareness of the role of night sky in protecting natural habitat, natural darkness and visibility of the night sky. The problem is that we are not teaching and people are not learning about the stars. People don't know their names. I connect the stars to the indigenous region of the straits while cruising on the Shepler ferry on the Straits of Mackinac. Night sky is an asset and resource that we can protect from light pollution. Paris France, 'The City of Lights' actually has a designated lighting engineer who rules on the way lights can be used so as to draw attention to the sites without disrupting the dark sky. The cruises were successful, so we changed the name to Shepler's Night Sky Cruises and added a few more cruises to the 2013 schedule, including a late-night meteor shower cruise that sold out days before the event. The meteor shower cruise was so popular that we have added a second cruise to the schedule in 2014 to view the Perseid meteor shower in August. Shepler's values our association with the Dark Sky Park at the Headlands, and we look forward to taking more and more visitors out every year to share in the beauty of the Straits of Mackinac, to watch the sun set, and to view the moon and the stars as they come out to grace the night sky."

Dick Moehl, Terry Pepper, and Mary Stuart Adams all had high praise for Shepler's willingness to help support their ideas and for their excellence in customer care. Terry had this to say, "As long as Shepler's conducts cruises, I will be there for them!"

Bill Shepler added, "The lighthouse cruises are an integral part of our goal of always doing what's best for the island. This is the kind of thing people want. For us, this is not related to money. It is much more about how can we contribute to providing the best possible experiences for those who live in or visit the Straits area in northern Michigan."

If seeing these lighthouses up close, and learning how they operate piques your interest, you can't go wrong by signing up for a lighthouse cruise. It's these kinds of special offerings that contribute to *Family Magazine* naming Mackinaw City "the number one family tourist town in America."

Shepler's Business Culture

In the early 1970s, a family trip to Disney World in Florida turned out to be one of the most important moves in Shepler's history. Bill was enormously impressed with the Disney operation: its handsomely costumed "cast" of workers, the attention to detail, the cleanliness and beauty of every area, and especially the employees' attitude toward their guests and eagerness to go the extra mile to please them. Bill went back again and again, taking advantage of the seminars Disney offered to businesspeople. Shepler's adopted many aspects of the Disney look: smart uniforms, two-way radios, name tags, and lavish landscaping.

When Bill Shepler visited Epcot Center, he noticed a sign on a door reading "cast members only." Intrigued, he investigated and saw that the red brick road and flower beds that led up to the door continued on the other side and that the backstage area was just as well-planned and attractive as the part of Epcot the public sees. There was a generous parking lot, a cafeteria with fresh food, and a pleasant break room. Bill realized that the backstage environment is just as important as the front because it shapes the attitude of the workers. They take the backstage environment—good or bad—with them when they're out in public. Bill envisioned Shepler's as a kind of Disney World North.

About this time, Shepler's bought a parcel of land just south of Mackinaw City, where they built a welcome center for Shepler's, Mackinaw City, and the island. The area was landscaped with grass, shrubs, and colorful flower beds and potted plants. Eventually, Shepler's entire area was beautifully landscaped. They hired a company called Polly's Plucking and Planting to handle the landscaping and sent owner Polly Cummings to Disney for a course in flowers and plantings. After Polly retired, Kim Clare "The Flower Lady" took over, and the Sheplers arranged for her to visit Disney World to study landscape technology, too. As of 2014, all of the flowers on the Shepler's docks and properties are planted and maintained by Barnwell Landscape and Garden Services, a Mackinac Island company specializing in plants by Proven Winners.

Jack Barnwell, owner, has the same vision as the Sheplers for the beauty of the property and the knowledge of the Disney look that they try to emulate.

Even more important than the outward manifestations was the Disney culture, an attitude toward the people who came to the park. They are seen as guests, not customers, and Disney intensively trains its staff to make sure those guests have a positive experience. According to the Shepler team:

"Our mantra is 'creating lasting memories.'" We go way beyond providing taxi service to and from Mackinac Island. Through our family-oriented personal service, attention to detail, humor, and special fun creations, we create lasting memories."

The Shepler's Mackinac Island Ferry Service has another distinct advantage: speed. Shepler's has, from the beginning, focused on having the fastest boats without sacrificing safety. Speed is a core competence for all leads and cast members and a clear source of competitive advantage for the Shepler's business. As Bill once jokingly said, "When you're skating on thin ice, your safety is in your speed!"

The Shepler's adaptation of the Disney culture is nurtured through the all-important yearly "Shepler's Traditions" training sessions. Says David Armour, "This training, and the culture it produces, has opened a huge competitive gap between Shepler's and their competition. The others often act as if they don't care if you ride or not. As a result, Shepler's has become the most successful ferry boat service, growing every year."

Attorney Ellen Crane wrote the Shepler training manual. Early in her career, she worked as a Shepler deck hand. She looks back fondly on the Shepler training program. According to Ellen, "The lessons I learned working for Shepler's helped me become successful in my career, as it did with many other Shepler student employees."

Ellen remembers how hard she worked, carrying luggage, wheeling passengers who are unable to walk across the ramp to and from the boat, and doing many other chores. Ellen remembers that the Sheplers were real sticklers with respect to customer care and safety. Ellen took great care in transporting handicapped passengers, trying hard to follow the training mandates. One day, however, she was wheeling a man backwards up the ramp from the boat dock to the boat. All of a sudden he started falling forward out of the wheelchair. As she looked on in horror, someone helped catch him. According to Ellen, "The man was all bug-eyed and upset!" She was relieved when Bill Shepler came to her rescue and calmed the man down. There was no complaint following the incident, but it did validate the value of the Shepler focus on customer service and safety.

Mackinaw Crossings

Just about the time that Chris and Bill were setting up their freight division, another exciting opportunity presented itself. Michigan Central Railroad had long since given up rail service to Mackinaw City, and in 1991, they made the move final by tearing up the tracks. Michigan Central had been responsible for much of the early growth of Mackinaw City and the island. Now, all that was left of its once-commanding position was thirty-six acres of land with a track bed, a sad, empty depot, and an old railroad dock that had been home to the railroad ferries, the *Chief Wawatam* and the *Santa Maria*.

Originally, Shepler's was only interested in the thirty-six acres of the railroad property, a large space for overflow parking, and the railroad dock to ensure they had space to maneuver their Travelift for launching. The Department of Natural Resources and Mackinaw City wanted the track bed, which they planned to turn into a trail area for hikers and snowmobilers. Bill Shepler tried to work out a deal for all of them with Cap Pinkerton, president and owner of the railroad. The DNR had first option on the land, but they dragged their feet. Mackinaw City didn't have the necessary money. Pinkerton wasn't interested in selling or leasing the dock separately. He set the price for the whole property at $2.5 million.

Tony Lieghio, who already owned nine Mackinaw City hotels, announced that he'd bought the property and planned to put a hotel or restaurant on the railroad dock, which would interfere with Shepler's launches from their own dock, just six feet away. Bill and Tony met, and Bill told Tony some things Tony hadn't known. For example, the dock rested on bottom lands, which are owned by the state. The state determines what can and cannot be done, and this particular bottom land was dedicated to marine use only. Upon verifying this information, Tony changed his mind about buying the railroad property. This opened the door for Bill to negotiate with the railroad property owners.

Soon after Tony informed the railroad property owners of his change of heart, the railroad's lead attorney contacted Bill and told him, "You and I can deal. How about $2.3 million? What can you put down?"

"Not much," Bill admitted. But Bill was intrigued. While most people saw the lonely, neglected depot as an eyesore, Bill saw it as an opportunity to turn Mackinaw City into a real destination instead of just a jumping-

off place for the island. Then Ira Green entered the picture. He was a developer from Petoskey whom Bill had known for some time. Ira became an active partner in the enterprise.

Bill had a big picture for turning the property into a center for entertainment, fine dining, and shopping, centered on the neglected but very picturesque depot. According to an article in the *Detroit Free Press,* Bill saw it as a kind of Disney World North, offering the Disney formula of excellent service, uniformed employees, business owners who saw themselves as hosts and hostesses, and the cleanliness and beauty that would bring people back again and again. Bill interested a group of forward-looking Mackinaw City businessmen in the concept. Bob Fisher, who owns the popular Pancake Chef restaurant, was one of them and says, "It was Bill's idea. Other people were involved, but he had the idea and worked hard for it."

In August of 1992, Bill spoke to a two-day seminar sponsored by the Mackinaw Area Tourist Bureau. Forty-five business owners listened as he told them how Mackinaw City would gain not only the new complex, which would be called Mackinaw Crossings, but also a new streetscape, including white lights at night similar to those of Disney World. Most of all, the employees of all Mackinaw City businesses would be trained to give super service. When Bill finished speaking, the entire audience stood and cheered. Gail McBride, executive director of the tourist bureau, said, "We hope that Mackinaw City and the Straits area will be the epitome of super service in Michigan. We are creating the new tourism. If we do it right, other communities will follow suit."

Bill Shepler and Bob Fisher developed a training program to improve the service culture in Mackinaw City. Bob tells how it began: "I was in a local gas station when a customer came in and said, 'Is there a place where I can rent a canoe?' The attendant didn't even look up—just said a flat 'No.' The customer left, and I followed him. He went over the bridge to St. Ignace. We had lost a customer. I was upset and called the visitors' bureau, and they put me in touch with Bill. We had similar ideas and attended seminars at Disney World. They make $1 million an hour down there. How can you argue with that kind of success? The training program we worked out was similar to the one Bill has used so successfully at the ferry service. We called it Service Magic, and it's had a lasting effect on the community. We stress the culture all the time and reinforce it with meetings and talks. It has changed the whole service attitude in Mackinaw City—our guests notice and comment."

Ira Green and architect Barry Polsen went to Disney World to soak up atmosphere and get ideas for the Crossings idea. Polsen came up with an eight-by-ten colored sketch showing what Mackinaw Crossings would look like. Bill took it to the bank after he signed a deal with the railroad. The bank loaned Bill $3.8 million to pay the railroad owners, develop, and clear the contamination on the property. The bank also agreed to allow Bill to sell off portions of the property to help pay off some of the debt. To help pay off the rest of the debt, the plan was to develop a portion of the land into a shopping and entertainment center. This plan would require partners to gain the assets to back up the bank note and to plan, build, and open the complex for business. Ira Green was very instrumental as a developer, as was the architect, Barry Polsen.

As the bank required, Bill and Ira found renters for 70 percent of the complex. This would allow them to restore the depot into a luxury dining space and construct the rest of the buildings.

And then the Odawa tribe from Petoskey announced some plans of its own. The tribe proposed to build a casino in Mackinaw City which would be open year-round and employ many local people. The town of Mackinaw City was torn: about half the people favored the new casino, and the other half were solidly against it. Occupancy of the still-unbuilt Crossings dropped to 30 percent as prospective shop owners feared that customers would flock to the casino instead of Crossings. In the end, the casino idea was turned down.

Bill and his partners had to regenerate interest in their project and get the rental level back to 70 percent. They did it. Contracts were signed, the money came from the bank, and construction started.

Excitement was running high. The grand opening was a gala event. Three thousand people turned out to watch Governor John Engler cut the ribbon and listen to his speech.

Ira Green had gone to Las Vegas and Branson to get ideas for a state-of-the-art theater. It seated 835 people and incorporated a fly system for scenery and a turntable. Greg Thompson came from Las Vegas to put on the shows. The first show featured singers, dancers, and a chorus line. On opening night, the chorus line turned around and displayed a row of bare bottoms, covered (if that's the word) only by thongs. It was controversial, to say the least. Someone pointed out that while Mackinaw City pasties and Las Vegas pasties are spelled the same, there's a world of difference between them. The next night, the chorus line was outfitted with bikini panties.

The first season was successful. The second season wasn't. The third year, a producer from Branson brought in shows from Las Vegas featuring old-time names like Mel Tillis and a group of Rat Pack impersonators. The theater made a $300,000 profit.

After that, the profits evaporated. Bill says, "We were spending money hand over fist. I wanted out." Crossings didn't turn out to be what he had dreamed of, and he realized that Mackinaw City hadn't turned into a destination city like Las Vegas or even Branson. People weren't coming, and attendance at the shows was really down.

The theater closed for good in 2006, and he finally decided to sell the whole place. Bill laments, "I thought that Crossings would work with Shepler's, but we couldn't open all those stores and staff them with people trained in the Shepler's customer-focused culture. We had to rent space out to people who just wouldn't buy into our concept of super service. We couldn't control their attitudes and how they ran their stores."

Jimmy Wehr, a partner and the new owner of the Crossings, gutted the theater and turned it into a Bass Pro sporting equipment store with an archery range and rock climbing wall. He lowered the rents and filled The Crossings with tenants. The old Michigan Central Depot is still there as a restaurant.

A friend of Bill's, Don Keller of Frankenmuth's Zehnder and Bavarian Inn operation, was fascinated by the Crossings concept. He hired Ira Green and commissioned him to design River Place in Frankenmuth.

The business woes caused by Crossings paled in comparison with the personal sorrows the family faced in the 1990s and 2000s. With age, Marge Shepler's health declined. Macular degeneration left her partially blind, and she became more and more frail. She was no longer able to take long walks, and the steep stairs to her apartment became a challenge. Bill installed a little elevator car to take her up and down. Marge died in 2004. She had lived a long, full life.

Bill and Suzanne's oldest daughter, Kathy, didn't have that chance. She preceded her grandmother in death in an automobile accident on March 10, 2000. This tragedy devastated the family. Billy says, "She had the biggest heart. A day doesn't go by I don't think of her. It makes me know life's too short—you can't be a grump."

Patty adored her big sister Kathy. "She was very bubbly and got along with everybody. She worked the most of any of us: she was manager of group sales, did the books, and also worked on the boats and docks. I can't believe the time has gone by. I keep thinking she's just on vacation."

Kathy, who had been married and divorced, left two little girls. Patty says, "Kathy's death had to be hardest on Ellyce and Mallory." Bill and Suzanne raised the girls. Mallory graduated from the University of Michigan, where she earned her degree in art and design. Ellyce graduated from Western Michigan University with a degree in family planning.

Chris, closest to Kathy in age, told an interviewer, "We had never been through anything like that before, and my parents' strength and our bonds made it easier somehow. Kathy had an upbeat sense of humor and a smile that would knock you down."

Chris remembers that impish sense of humor with a smile. "Dad was once bringing money from the ticket office in a big Maxwell House coffee can when someone wanted fuel for his boat. Dad put the coffee can on a fuel pump and forgot it. Kathy went down and picked it up. Then when he came upstairs, she asked him, all innocent, 'Where's the coffee can, Dad?' She really had him going."

Saving the Mackinaw

One good thing came out of the whole Crossings debacle. Shepler's retained the railroad dock and a large tract of land, which would play a vital role in a dramatic rescue. For sixty-two years, the United States Coast Guard Cutter *Mackinaw* was the most beloved vessel on the Great Lakes. It wasn't just that the *Mackinaw* was famous for delivering Christmas trees to needy youngsters in Chicago or serving as an escort for both the Port Huron to Mackinac and the Chicago to Mackinac sailing races. There was much more. She was a popular part of community activities, including the annual Coast Guard Festival in Grand Haven and visits of tall ships to the Lakes. The cutter's ice-breaking capabilities were amazing: when an ice-bound crew saw the big boat circle and start tossing three-foot chunks of ice around like ice cubes, they probably thought it was one of the most beautiful sights they'd ever witnessed.

From the beginning, the *Mackinaw* was special. Until World War II, the Great Lakes had never had a real icebreaker, although various areas had boats with some icebreaking ability. In the Straits, *Chief Wawatam,* the big railroad ferry, was such a vessel. Also, certain captains were especially talented when it came to getting a boat out of the ice. The first William Schepler had that ability. When a boat got stuck, they'd send a crew member to slog his way across the ice and knock on his door. William would throw on his heavy jacket and galoshes and go to the rescue. He was often able to free the boat. According to Ken Teysen, the choice was between William and dynamite.

The war effort demanded an uninterrupted supply of iron ore, limestone, and coal to make steel for weapons, planes, tanks, and ships, but the lakes were iced over for several months each winter. A really powerful icebreaker was needed to keep the freighters and their precious supplies going. Ten days after Pearl Harbor, Congress authorized the construction of the best, largest, and most powerful icebreaker in the world. Legislators from the Great Lakes states, afraid that the new boat would be taken over for the war effort in other parts of the world, paid particular attention to the dimensions of the cutter. Michigan Congressman Bradley made sure that it was too big to fit through the pre-1959 Welland Canal.

The *Mackinaw* was designed by naval architects Gibbs and Cox. The keel was laid March 20, 1943, at the Toledo Shipbuilding Company. When that company went broke, the job was taken over by the Cleveland-based American Shipbuilding and Drydock Company. A variation of the Coast Guard's WIND-class polar icebreaker, she is one of a kind. Mackinaw is longer than other WIND vessels, has a wider beam and a shallower draft, and is especially designed to work in the Great Lakes. Also, the cooling system is built to use fresh water, not salt. She is designed to go through three feet of blue ice at four knots.

The icebreaker has a bow propeller that pulls water away from the ice. The ice becomes sort of an unsupported shelf which allows the icebreaker, through its sheer weight and power, to crush the shelf of ice below its bow. Thick steel plating protects the hull.

It is important to note that the current technology of "bow propeller" icebreaking was discovered by Captain Boyton, of St. Ignace. Sometime in the late 1890s, he received plea for help to rescue a ship that was stuck in the ice in the Alpena Harbor. For some unknown reason, he took not one, but two ships to try to free the ice-locked ship. Upon arriving at the harbor, he found that he couldn't get in, so he arranged the boats bow to stern and latched them together so that there was a bow propeller and a stern propeller side by side. These two boats essentially functioned as one. The modern approach to crushing the ice, as used by the *Mackinaw* icebreaker, was born.

Having the capacity to cut through three-foot of blue ice or five foot of brash (fragmented, refrozen ice), she can circle a thousand-foot vessel stuck in thirty-two inches of solid ice in thirty minutes.

With a fuel oil capacity of 276,000 gallons, the *Mackinaw* has a range of 41,000 nautical miles at 11 knots. She displaces 5,252 tons, is 290 feet long and 74'5" wide, and draws 19'2". Her six Fairbanks-Morse 2,000-hp diesel engines are each connected to an electric generator which in turn drives three 5,000-hp motors that provide the main propulsion to the two stern propellers and the bow propeller. They gave the *Mac* a maximum speed of 20 knots and the ability to tow 120,000 pounds. She has two 6,000-pound anchors with two-inch-diameter links and carries eight officers and sixty-seven enlisted men. Her half-football shape makes her immediately recognizable, and she cost $10 million to build.

The *Mackinaw* was commissioned on December 20, 1944, just in time to escort three new 4,000-ton freighters through heavy ice out of the Lakes. It was the first of hundreds of escort and rescue operations. The *Mackinaw* symbolized the American fighting spirit of the WWII war effort. She helped win the war by keeping the Great Lakes open in the winter, allowing transport of iron ore from  Duluth, Minnesota to Chicago, Illinois and Gary, Indiana. She simply could not be stopped.

After the war, the *Mackinaw* continued to play a vital role in Great Lakes commerce. For instance, in 1948, she was called to the Buffalo area of Lake Erie where twelve vessels were ice locked. She freed them all.

She was mostly called the *Mackinaw* or *Big Mac,* but admirers also called her the Guardian of the Lakes and the Great White Mother. However, the paint color was changed from white to a brilliant crimson to make her more visible against the ice, and the Great Red Mother just didn't have the same ring to it.

Age finally caught up with the Guardian of the Lakes. She was just worn out and had become very expensive and difficult to maintain. For instance, the complicated engine system required a group of fourteen highly specialized experts to keep her running.

The Coast Guard first planned to replace her in the early 1990s. After the Coast Guard formally announced the decommissioning, the Icebreaker Mackinaw Maritime Museum Association (IMMM) was formed by a group of Cheboygan residents who had a deep affection for the vessel and for keeping the vessel in Cheboygan. It was assumed that it would take in excess of a million dollars to build an appropriate mooring dock in the Cheboygan River. After about three years, it became apparent that the association was having extreme difficulty in raising the necessary funds to fulfill this objective.

In the meantime, Bill Shepler and his friends Dick Moehl and Sandy Planisek became extremely interested in saving the vessel. Shepler's owned the old railroad dock formerly used to moor the icebreaker and railroad ferry *Chief Wawatam*, which would provide the deep draft needed for the *Mackinaw*. It was located in downtown Mackinaw City and would therefore provide easy access for the many tourists who visit Mackinaw City.

The Coast Guard delayed her decommissioning, but eventually a new *Mackinaw* was ordered and built. The new icebreaker was equipped with the latest electronic, communications, and icebreaking equipment and can also double as a buoy tender. Azipods provide the main propulsion to the 240-foot cutter. Combined with a 550-hp bow thruster, the Azipods make the new *Mackinaw* very maneuverable. Built by the Marinette Machine Corp, she carries nine officers and forty-six enlisted men, far fewer than the first *Mackinaw*.

There were others besides Bill, Dick, and Sandy who were interested in the fate of the beloved old cutter. Several communities wanted her for a museum. They included Duluth, Minnesota, whose ore boats the *Mackinaw* had kept running, Grand Haven, Michigan, and her home port of Cheboygan, which the Coast Guard had identified as having first priority, should it be able to generate the necessary funds.

The groups that wanted the *Mackinaw* had to prove that they had a berth for her plus the funds and ability to maintain her. Duluth and Grand

Haven dropped out. Cheboygan regretfully dropped out of the running when they found they couldn't raise a million dollars to provide docking facilities. After the Cheboygan group dropped out, Bill, Dick Moehl, and Sandy Planesik formed a Mackinaw City association to petition the Coast Guard for the *Mackinaw*.

Bill said, "It was simple. We had a deep dock and adequate space for the *Mackinaw*. It was necessary to save the vessel, as she stands for 'the America that will never quit, always win, and always help.' She is one of the few vessels that were designed to do a job, and she did it."

Another plus for the Mackinaw City location was access to the services of Shepler's crack team of mechanics. This team winterized her the first year, using six hundred gallons of antifreeze to protect the water system. In the winter months, a team member goes aboard once a week to check her out and make sure nothing's leaking.

Jeff Beach, the Coast Guard's decommissioned boat manager, said, "The Coast Guard's property staff worked eighteen months to find a good home for the Mackinaw. Without the Shepler's pier being made available, the Coast Guard would have been forced to move the ship to the Coast Guard shipyard in Baltimore, knowing that the salt water transit would cause potential damage to the vessel's engine cooling system. It probably wouldn't have been able to leave Baltimore under its own power and would have had to be scrapped."

The *Mackinaw* was decommissioned on June 10, 2006, at the Olds Memorial Mooring in Cheboygan. The new *Mackinaw* was commissioned on the same day. It was an impressive gala but bittersweet. Commandant Thad Allen was joined by a group of dignitaries which included Jean Hastert, sponsor of the new *Mackinaw*, her husband, Congressman Dennis Hastert, and Bart Stupak of Michigan's First Congressional District. There were also former officers and crew members of the *Mackinaw*, including Commander Joe McGinnnis. The Coast Guard band, from the Academy in New London, played. As the last skipper of the *Mackinaw* and its last crew left the ship, there wasn't a dry eye in the tent. The audience was deeply moved by Commander Joe McGinnis's moving tribute, "She was a heavyweight fighter who never lost a fight. She always won."

The new IMMM committee had made plans for the *Mackinaw*'s final voyage from Cheboygan to Mackinaw City. The committee wanted to sell tickets for the trip in order to raise money for the ship's maintenance. They were informed that it was illegal to charge the seven hundred planned passengers for transportation on a Coast Guard vessel and that they would need to come up with seven hundred life jackets. It didn't take them long to solve that problem. The group was traveling from Mackinaw City to Cheboygan on buses, so they charged for the bus ride instead.

It took almost a year and over $200,000 to change the Mackinaw from a working ship to a museum. Lisa Pallagi heads a staff of twenty-five volunteers who give tours, welcome people aboard, do maintenance, and work in the gift shop. The tours are designed to give the visitor a sensory experience of what it must have been like when the *Mackinaw* was serving our country. The hope is that the experience will in some ways rekindle the fighting spirit and American pride of the post–World War II years. Tours last about forty-five minutes and include the pilot house, the engine room, the library, the mess hall, the bridge, the executive officer's quarters, and the bunk areas. The visitors count averages between twenty and twenty-two thousand people each season. The Icebreaker Mackinaw Maritime Museum is open for tours from May through September. The process of installing water and sewage facilities is underway. This will allow for a reopening of the mess hall to better accommodate overnight groups like Boy Scout troops.

Leading Roles

Bill, Chris, Patty, and Billy have assembled a team of "leads" and "cast" members to serve their guests. Shepler's leads and ship captains are the acknowledged stars of the cast. Who are they and what do they do? The information and training manual says, "Leads are chosen for their superior qualifications, for their ability to command and to direct." The lead position is a step up because they become part of management. The job also carries added responsibility. The manual reads, "The lead's job is a demanding one, and the lead must be perceptive, thinking all the time, constantly on the move." The ship captains are, like airline pilots, the navigational and safety experts the customers put their faith in.

Jason Wiley has an extremely important position. He is not only human resources director (as described in "Joining the Shepler's Crew") but is also head dock master, which often means that he's the face of Shepler's. Jason started out working in the parking lot, directing guests where to park and moved up to deckhand and eventually became a captain. Jason maintains his captain's license, but enjoys his work on the dock. He works a minimum of ten hours a day, six days a week. Those days are very full. He's in charge of all the dock workers in Mackinaw City as well as the deck hands when they're in port. That means he's responsible for scheduling and directing about sixty people. He checks out their appearance, makes sure they're on time and in place, and tells them exactly what they're supposed to do. He, along with other supporting leads, is charge of getting cars and buses unloaded and making sure the baggage is properly tagged and packed on carts. They need to be in constant communication with all departments, so they use onshore communication equipment such as cell phones and two-way VHF radios that have a nine channel capacity to connect with the car care, freight, dock, and marine service divisions. This radio system is invaluable to the Shepler culture.

Jason is the ultimate traffic director on the dock. Cars, RVs, and buses have to be parked in the proper lots, and he has to know the location of every vehicle. Sometimes a guest with an expensive new car wants two parking spaces or a place in the shade. Jason just can't make exceptions like that. If all the guests parked where they wanted, it would be absolute chaos.

He also deals with guests, making sure they know where to buy tickets and board. He announces arrivals and departures of the ferries and answers dozens of questions every day. If a crew member can't solve a guest issue, the problem goes to Jason.

Jason explained how earning the Grand Hotel account has affected the Shepler's business. According to Jason, "When the Grand Hotel began using Shepler's as its preferred ferry service to Mackinac Island in 2010, our business exploded overnight. The Grand is especially phenomenal with its use of social media to attract guests in the fall. I estimate that they have an average of 180 to 200 rooms checking in and out every day from May through October, all traveling with Shepler's."

The dock lead on Mackinac Island is Damian Mendez. He deals with the hotel dock porters, which can be difficult since they're not part of the Shepler's crew. They are hired by the various hotels, inns, and bed and-breakfasts to deliver their guests' luggage. Shepler's has a code regarding conduct, appearance, attitude, and how to handle the guests and their luggage. The Mackinac Island lead enforces this code and has the authority to remove dock porters from the dock for any misconduct. When guests are leaving the island, he collects their car claim checks and scans them for St. Ignace and Mackinaw City so their cars will be waiting on the dock when they get off the ferry.

Armand Horn is the St. Ignace General Manager. He has been with Shepler's since 1997, starting out as a deck hand. The St. Ignace Dock has less volume than the Mackinaw City Dock. According to Armand, "This is a benefit to the guests in that there is much less congestion—more elbow room." Armand adds, "I say that St. Ignace is the best-kept secret in the Straits. It is absolutely beautiful, and it doesn't have the massive crowds that they contend with in Mackinaw City."

A story about the handling of one problem illustrates how leads handle difficult situations. One day, a couple came to the St. Ignace Dock. The husband gave his wife money to pay for their ferry tickets and parking. The problem started when the ticket seller was distracted with another guest's question and put the bill in the cash drawer before making change, forgetting that she'd been trained to always put the bill on top of the drawer until she counted the change back into the customer's hand. After the couple arrived at the Island, the husband asked his wife for the change and she handed him $14. "But I gave you a hundred-dollar bill!" he protested. They found Annie Bentley, and the husband erupted, yelling a stream of four-letter words. Annie took over. Very calmly she promised, "If we're over when we count the cash tonight, I'll bring you the money." Mollified but still muttering, they went on their way. Sure enough, the cash was over that evening. Annie took their change and walked to Mission Point Resort to return their money. Leads are expected to go the extra mile. This level of customer service attitude reflects the Shepler's way of meeting and exceeding customer expectations. Incidentally, Annie later married another Shepler's lead, one of several such marriages over the years.

The current St. Ignace dock lead is Courtney Inglis, the daughter of Captain Mark Inglis. She was first hired as a high-school student to park cars for the Mackinaw City guests. She was promoted several times, from handling dock luggage to serving as a deck hand on the boats and then working as valet lead in Mackinaw City and dock lead at St. Ignace—all within an eight-year period. This progress is rather typical of the career ladder opportunities at Shepler's if you work hard, are a good team player, and exude the Shepler's cultural values and behaviors.

The maintenance staff is currently headed by Andrew Ming. Andrew has been with the Shepler organization for twelve years. Andrew heads a crew of ten who make sure the docks, ferries, restrooms, and parking lots are always immaculate. He starts every morning scheduling shifts and duties, ordering cleaning and restroom supplies, and checking the boats to be sure the night crew did a good job. He opens the restrooms and the cast rooms where members of the various crews take their breaks and eat lunch. The restrooms get special attention. Andrew's staff checks each restroom and break room at least once an hour to ensure they're always clean and well-stocked. Shepler's restrooms were built in 2002 with quality in mind. They are large and barrier-free, with stainless steel stalls, Corion countertops, automatic flush toilets, tiled floors and ceilings, air conditioning, and heat from the floor, so it is always dry and warm. Andrew and his crew cut the grass, repair and paint when necessary, and maintain equipment of all kinds. The docks need constant attention: people drop candy, gum wrappers, and often spill drinks. Finally, if the dock area gets too full of cars, the custodians lend a hand with overnight car parking. The overall goal is to ensure that everything is clean and presentable, looking brand new for the guests. Belief in Shepler's culture is a key reason employees work for Shepler's rather than the other ferry lines.

The head transportation lead is Greg Pietrowski. He recently replaced Dennis Wysocki. Greg is in charge of scheduling the vans and busses that transport guests to and from hotels, motels, and campgrounds to the ferry dock.

A major responsibility of the transportation department is the maintenance and repair of Shepler's shuttle fleet: four fifteen-passenger vans, three twenty-one-passenger minibuses, a 17 passenger accessible bus with lift mechanisms that can accommodate 3 wheelchairs, and one eighty-passenger tram.

Shepler's also provides the drivers for the Grand Hotel's beautiful classic 1959 Cadillac Limousine to chauffeur Grand Hotel VIP guests. They also store and maintain the limousine for Grand Hotel. Incidentally, this limousine was once used as a security vehicle for transporting Mamie Eisenhower. All of the vehicles are kept in top running condition and vacuumed and washed at least once every day. The vehicles pick up guests from St. Ignace and Mackinaw City hotels, motels, and campgrounds and take them to the ferry docks.

To arrange for a shuttle pickup, the guest or the hotel desk clerk calls Shepler's main office. The dispatcher passes all relevant information on to the proper bus or van driver. Each bus and van has been equipped with a computerized, dash-mounted communication system. It facilitates quick and easy communication between the dispatcher and each driver. This system replaces the old radio system that was at times unreliable and cumbersome. The shuttle dispatcher sends the right-sized vehicle and tells the hotel when it will arrive. When the guests get back from the island, they're shuttled back to their lodging. There is no bother with cars or parking. It's a popular free service that benefits the guests and means less congestion on the dock.

Dennis points out, "As the drivers, we pave the way for the guests to get off to the best possible start in experiencing Shepler's friendliness and efficiency. We are both the beginning and the end of a great experience that leaves guests smiling and wanting to come back. During the drive time, we also act as a kind of concierge service, answering questions about what to see, where to eat, or what to do on the island. I am so proud of my crew because they are always willing to go the extra mile for our guests—for instance, going back to pick up things like cameras that a guest forgot back at the hotel. Within the Shepler organization, this attitude is pervasive."

Tom Bushman is the car care center lead in charge of the secured parking lots, which offer inside and outside secured parking for over five hundred cars. Most of cars in the inside secured parking are late-model, luxury or classic cars. What if one of those beauties gets a scratch or a dent? It almost never happens; perhaps three or four cars are damaged out of the forty-five thousand that are handled every summer. When it does happen, Tom Bushman, the car care lead, meets with the guest, goes over the damage, fills out the form, and it gets turned over to Shepler's insurance company. Once in a while, someone will try to pull a fast one by blaming an attendant for a scratch that was there before, but each car is checked as it comes in, and any damage is noted.

Nine cast members work under Tom's direction. Most of these cast members are retired from lifelong jobs. "These guys are reliable," says Tom. "They're always on time, and they're absolutely trustworthy."

In 1972, Dustin's Garage and Gas Station was bought and equipped to handle bus service with a wash rack and restroom dump facility. This reflected the growth of the group tour market. Shepler's has been a leader in the American Bus Association, the National Tour Association, and the Ontario Motor Coach Association, all representing different segments of group travel.

Misty Martinchek, Director of Sales and Marketing, recalls an especially challenging group transfer. "A group of 300 people in 150 motorhomes was staying at one of the Mackinaw City campgrounds. We're used to offering shuttle service to individuals and groups, but a group that big should have set it up in advance. They didn't, and we didn't find out about them until the day before they wanted to go to the Island. They couldn't be staggered because they had a carriage tour of the island set up for a certain time. I got busy trying to figure out what to do. We had another group scheduled to come to the dock from the Pellston airport just about the time the motorhome people were supposed to be picked up. They had rented coaches from Traverse City. I called the Traverse City company and asked if we could use their coaches. They agreed, and that took care of ninety people. There were 210 to go. Then I called the trolley company here in Mackinaw City and lined up two trolleys. At the time, our own fleet consisted of one bus, holding thirty people, and two vans that each held fifteen. We still had 110 to go. I was really casting around, trying to think of something else. Finally, I remembered that we had two groups of school kids who were scheduled to stay overnight on the island. That meant that their buses would be staying in our parking lot. I called both companies and asked to rent the buses for one hour. Everyone was just great," adds Misty, "and we managed to get all those three hundred people to the island on time."

A graduate of Indiana University, Misty works with all kind of groups to plan their Mackinac Island adventures. There are conventions, weddings, school groups, and tour groups—over one thousand groups every year. Misty is also in charge of online sales, Internet marketing, and advertising. "We reach our customers by billboards, the Internet, radio ads, newspaper ads, brochures, industry magazines, and occasional use of television ads."

One special perk for Misty is going with Chris to travel shows where they meet and talk to tour operators. Shows have been held in Toronto, New York City, Chicago, Virginia Beach, Dallas, and Nashville. In 1981, Bill Shepler and some associates formed Circle Michigan to help tour operators, group leaders, and schools plan successful trips based on Michigan attractions. Bill served as president for three years and was on the board for many years. Misty has also served as president and is currently on the board of directors.

Sue LaCross is the office manager. An accountant, Sue started in 1988 and has seen a lot of changes over the years. "When I started, we were in a very small office. Since then, we've gone to a much bigger office and our accounting staff has grown to five. We used to deal strictly in cash, but now we take credit cards and sell tickets online. That meant getting new phone lines and new credit card terminals."

One of the biggest changes has been the online sale of tickets and parking, which Chris initiated in 2004. Sue says, "It's a good tool. If people have already bought their tickets, they don't change their minds when they see a billboard for another ferry line." What about Canadian money? Sue says, "We get a lot, especially in St. Ignace, but that's no problem. I check the discount rate with the bank at least once a week, sometimes every day."

Greg Torsky was the first manager of Captain Bill's Espresso and Coffee Bar on the dock in Mackinaw City. Before that, he was manager of a beer and wine distributorship in Petoskey for twenty-seven years. Greg has now been succeeded by Kathleen Winch. Greg still works when needed, but is enjoying all the perks of retirement. The coffee bar was started as the modern recreation of Mrs. Shepler's snack bar, the Quarterdeck. Kathleen heads a team of four who sell coffee, cold espresso drinks, hot chocolate, pop, bottled water, a variety of sandwiches, subs, soups, pizza, candy, and chips, as well as, film, T-shirts, umbrellas, and raincoats. It's open from May 1 to the end of October, from seven a.m. to three p.m. During the peak season (June 20–September 1), they serve three to four hundred guests a day, and customers have included Bob Hope, Bob Seger, Governor John Engler, and rock star Kid Rock. Kathleen's other duties include marketing, merchandise, ordering, and inventory control. In the spring and fall, she helps out on the dock, doing valet parking, handling luggage, and "everything that needs doing." In the fall, especially, everyone does whatever is called for.

Bob Darrow has been a cast member for over thirty-five years and heads Shepler's Marine Service, which got started with the speedboats. Bill Shepler recalls, "We needed a place to store our boats in the winter and work on them. At first, we just hauled them out and covered them with canvas; we had to work in the rain and snow. When we got the first cruiser, the local crane was too small to handle them, so Cap found a boathouse in Cheboygan. It had been used to house a couple of high-speed boats during Prohibition and had two haul-out winches. It was a great improvement, but it wasn't heated and was cold in the winter. After we bought the railroad property, we put up a pole barn and bought a twelve-ton Travelift. The building was big enough to store eight or nine other boats. About that time, he also hired a mechanic and a fiberglass specialist. The Travelift could only lift twelve tons, and both ends were closed, so it couldn't raise a sailboat or a power boat with a big cabin. This is when Bill and Cap decided that there was a need for a marina in Mackinaw City. Ford Martin, a marine contractor, was employed to build a ramp to accommodate over a hundred tons, and they bought an eighty-five-ton Travelift that could lift just about any yacht in the Great Lakes.

In 1975, they added another building that included a large paint room and the Ship Store, which was just a 25'-x-14' section of the Marine Building. The store was so popular that in 1992, they built an 850-square-foot addition. The store offers boating apparel, charts, and marine supplies, and Marine Service offers everything from an oil change and maintenance to complete repowering and refinishing. They do fiberglass and gel-coat repairs and refinishing, wood repairs and varnishing, polishing, waxing, and painting.

Shepler's uses AwlGrip, a very hard surface paint used to paint aircraft. Shepler's cabins and hulls are painted every six to eight years. Aft decks and stairwell areas are painted every year. The paint costs $100 a quart.

Bob Darrow tells boaters, "You won't find a more accommodating bunch anywhere in the Great Lakes. We know your boat is your baby, and we'll treat it like it was our own."

The Marine Service is open from eight a.m. to five p.m., seven days a week, from May till October. Marine Service also rents equipment, including hydraulic trailers, forklifts, welders with operators, and trucks.

Charlie Socolovitch supervises five mechanics that are known as absolutely the best in the Straits area. Longtime Shepler friend and attorney Judge William Crane says, "Bill always has a spare engine on the shelf: if one of his boats breaks down, he can have it back and running in four hours. When something goes wrong with another ferry company's boats, Shepler's has the facilities to be able to haul their boats out of the water for repair."

Charlie's crew does repairs and preventive maintenance on Shepler's fleet, the 250 private yachts they store in the winter, plus boats in transit in the summer. Among those summer visitors have been Gordon Lightfoot and Bob Segar. Chuck Norris and Walter Peyton came in for fuel and work on their engine when they were taking part in an offshore Chicago-Detroit race.

Shepler's mechanics are certified to work on gas and diesel engines, including Detroit Diesel, Yanmar, and Mercruiser. They also take care of pump, transmission and prop problems, and just about anything that can go wrong. Says Charlie, "Sometimes a boat will be sinking as it pulls in; sometimes shafts are ripped right out when a boat hits bottom. I make sure they're up to speed and safe by the time they leave." Charlie wants every job to be perfect; every vessel in Shepler's fleet is checked by a mechanic and cleaned every morning. Their biggest job was lengthening the *Capt. Shepler,* the *Wyandot,* and the *Hope* and totally repowering them with

1,400-horsepower MTU Detroit Diesel engines. This whole transformation was prompted by the increase in Shepler's passenger business.

Charlie grew up at Shepler's, starting when he was in high school back in 1980. He's part of three generations of the Socolovitch family that has worked at Shepler's. His dad, Edward, started working as a welder and mechanic in the 1970s. Charley's brother Steve, also a welder, helped design and build the first of many luggage carts for Shepler's Mackinac Island Ferry. Charlie's son Tyler and his daughter Holly and Steve's two sons, Blake and Dylan, currently work at Shepler's.

In addition to supervising the mechanics, Charlie is also a professional scuba diver. When *Wyandot* and *Capt. Shepler* developed cavitation problems, Charlie went down to film the propeller operation with an underwater camera to help solve the problems. He also does work for the Bay View Yacht Club during the Bay View to Mackinac Island sailboat races. He goes out on the *Sacre Bleu* and sets a buoy by dropping and positioning a thousand-pound concrete block to hold the finish line buoy in place. "I work on top of the water and also under," he says.

Bill Crane shared a story that serves as an example of how Shepler's takes care of its customers. According to Crane, "I brought a 1961 Chris Craft Sea Skiff to Shepler's for maintenance and storage in 1974. I asked Bill Shepler if he could recommend a good name for the boat. He allowed me to use one of the names made available to him that consisted of the former names of early vessels. We chose the name, 'Adventure.' Over the years, Shepler's replaced several ribs and planks, an engine, and a transmission—and applied a lot of varnish to keep the *Adventure* going. In August 2009, while in transit on the *Adventure* from Cheboygan to St. Helena, I laid the *Adventure* in at the Mackinaw City dock.

"When I came back that Saturday night, to my horror I saw that the *Adventure* was starting to sink, much like the Titanic—bow down and stern up. I quickly found out that my bilge pump was not working and that the boat would soon sink if I didn't get help. I desperately began calling people in hopes of borrowing a bilge pump. I talked to the dock master, the sheriff's department, the police department, and the fire department, but none had an available bilge pump. My call to the Coast Guard went unanswered, as they were out patrolling the areas in and around the bridge.

"Shepler's Marine had long since closed, but I managed to get hold of Bill Shepler on his home phone. I told him that I was convinced that the *Adventure* was going down. Bill swung into action, calling the five dock hands that were waiting to receive the last ferry from the Island and sending all of them to the rescue. We started a bucket brigade, bailing furiously.

"Meanwhile, Bill Shepler had called his maintenance lead, Andrew Ming, who raced over with a Shop-vac. That drew enough water out to somewhat stabilize the boat. Bill Shepler also called Charlie Socolovitch, who was enjoying himself at a Saturday night party. Charley immediately left the party and joined the rescue mission, which by now had drawn a crowd of observers, including the fire and police departments. After Charley arrived, we started the engines, turned on all of the lights, including the half-mile search light, blew the horns, and navigated slowly around the gas dock and into the hands of Charlie at the boat hoist.

"The *Adventure* survived! As has been the case before, with many other devoted customers, Shepler's crew went the extra mile to save a precious boat—and build lifelong loyalty to his business."

Every January, Bill, Billy, Chris, and Patty meet with the leads for a retreat. They go over the budget and projections, and they discuss what was done right and wrong in the past year and what can be done better in the year ahead. They always keep in mind that Shepler's sets the standard for the industry.

Each of Shepler's captains is the undisputed boss of his domain while on the water. Shepler's training manual states, "The captains are in command of the ships. Whatever they say goes. They are expected to follow, as close as possible, the policies and procedures outlined by management. They have authority to make decisions in regard to the operation of their vessel—weather, speed, sea conditions, etc. Management cannot predict every situation, so the captains have the authority to decide what is best for their boats. They are primarily concerned for the safety of the people on board. With that goes the safe operation of the vessels."

In "A Visit to Mackinac Island" you will meet Captain Erik Heffernan. Nearly all of the crossings are uneventful, but the captains and their crews always have to be prepared for any emergency. He and all of the Shepler's captains are responsible for safety procedures related to fire, man overboard, running aground, collision with another vessel, sinking and mechanical failure.

In addition to Captain Erik, Shepler's has ten other captains: Mark Inglis, Bill Shepler, Chris Shepler, Fleet Captain Billy Shepler, Greg Bawol, Tom Markham, Jason Wiley, Pat Springate, Geoff Hoeksema, and Rick Weaver.

Former captain Kevin Coe worked as a deckhand for five years while he was attending Grand Valley State University. He became an accountant but found he hated working with figures in an office. He came back to Shepler's and got his captain's license in 2001. Kevin lost two fingers and part of his left hand in an accident aboard the *Wyandot*. He tells what happened next. "I got off the boat, and Bill was coming down the dock. I went up to him with my hand streaming with blood and said, 'This has ruined my day.' Bill went into action, called for ice and towels, and contacted the state police for an escort. On the way, he called the hospital to let them know we were coming. We made it to Cheboygan in record time. I was still in the emergency room when my mother arrived. She looked at me and said, 'You'd do *anything* to get out of doing the dishes!'"

Kevin adds, 'The lawyers came out of the woodwork, but I didn't sue. I'm not disabled. I love my work—it's my dream." Pointing to the view from the bridge of the *Welcome*, he says, "I have the most beautiful office in northern Michigan. I whistle on my way to work every day."

Kevin and his wife were offered high-paying jobs in Las Vegas but turned them down. "I don't think they have ferries on Lake Mead," he says. "It's a quality of life issue. There's nothing else I'd rather do."

Captain Mark Inglis started as a deckhand right out of Cheboygan High School and has been with Shepler's since 1985. Like all the other captains, he's fascinated by the ever-changing weather in the Straits. He also loves the view from his "window," enjoys interacting with passengers, and likes the fact that every day offers different challenges. He also enjoys an occasional battle with Mother Nature. She won at least one. Mark usually drives the *Felicity* between St. Ignace and the island. "When I left the island, I went over fourteen-to-fifteen-foot waves, but I was doing okay until I hit the Three Sisters. The Three Sisters are three huge bogus waves, one right after another. I just couldn't control the boat, and I had to go back and tie up at the Island." Mark felt a little better when he found out that some of the big boys—nine-hundred-to-thousand-foot freighters—also had to anchor at St. Ignace to wait out the stormy sea.

Mark was driving *Felicity* on a tragic day in 1989 when a young woman, anxious to meet her boyfriend in the Upper Peninsula and hurrying, went off the bridge in her Yugo. It was the only such accident in the fifty-year-plus history of the bridge, and Mark remembers it vividly. "It was a normal rough day," Mark recalls. "Winds were about fifty miles per hour, and there were ten-to-twelve-foot waves. In minutes, the whole area was filled with Coast Guard helicopters and rescue boats, but the Yugo had gone to the bottom. They didn't find it until much later."

During the winter months, Mark sometimes works in Marine Service, helping Bob Darrow sand and paint the ferry boats. He also does general maintenance and waxes and buffs the private boats in storage. His daughter Courtney worked with him on the Felicity as a deckhand before being promoted. His daughter Carin has worked on the dock and the parking lot. His wife, Teresa, worked at Shepler's in the late eighties and then again in recent years in the St. Ignace Ticket Office.

Fleet Captain Billy Shepler has his own weather stories. "I like most weather, and I especially like watching the sunrise. That's even better than the sunset. I even like bad weather, but sometimes it gets a little too bad. One day I saw squalls and dense clouds on the radar, and I knew we had weather coming. We got into Mackinaw City. I thought we could make it to the island and tie up, but the storm engulfed us. We were heading east-northeast to the island, the wind was out of the northwest, and we were being blown toward Cheboygan. I turned the ferry into the wind, but it kept moving us sideways. Once the squall went past, I found we'd been blown two and a half miles off course in just five minutes. The storm was unbelievable and humbling. I never saw a storm like that! And then the sun came out. I looked at the crew and said, 'What happened?'"

Billy cherishes another weather memory. "It was a fall day with high wind and fifteen-foot waves. About five p.m., I came around the Round Island and looked up at the south tower of the bridge. It was illuminated by a hole in the clouds where the sun shone through. A big wave hit the tower, and there was a brilliant rainbow of colors in the spray. Mother Nature, God, and I were the only ones who saw it."

Joining the Shepler Crew

The hiring process for the Shepler's Mackinac Island Ferry Service begins in November, but applications begin arriving during the previous summer. Most employees come via the Internet (see sheplersferry.com), and applicants range from high school students to senior citizens looking for a second career after retirement. The majority are attending college.

Patty Janes, formerly a Professor of Recreation, Parks, and Leisure Services Administration at Central Michigan University, worked with Shepler's, telling qualified students about opportunities at the ferry service. Each February, Shepler's participates in CMU's summer employment day, and Bill and Chris lecture to Dr. Janes's marketing classes. She included the Shepler's story when she wrote a marketing textbook and is enthusiastic about the success of Shepler's culture. "They have high expectations for their employees," she says. "They always expect a professional look and a professional attitude. They place great emphasis on quality, and they want people who can deliver great service. Also, they're good people to work for because they believe in serving both their guests and their employees." Dr. Janes points out that many of her students have been able to acquire permanent jobs due to the training they received at Shepler's.

After reading through as many as two thousand applications, Shepler's human resource team selects 400-500 for personal interviews. In addition to good grades and a clean-cut appearance, they look for extracurricular activities, athletics, sports, clubs, and community involvement. During the interviews, candidates learn about the hardest aspects of the jobs. They learn that they will work in all kinds of weather doing physically strenuous activities. The goal is to hire those who are committed to working and are excited about the job. The Sheplers hire tough because they want the best. Of the hundreds interviewed, approximately thirty to forty new workers are typically hired each summer to make up the summer crew of 180. There are also fifty full-time employees.

The addition of the Grand Hotel account triggered a major change in Shepler's hiring. The huge increase in fall business made Shepler's rethink their entire hiring model. For decades, they had relied on college help, but the typical college student must return to school in mid-August. In an effort to remedy this situation, Andrew Ming, the maintenance lead, went on a hiring trip to Jamaica in February of 2013. While there, he interviewed roughly forty applicants and hired fifteen. Jamaica has a very strong pool of applicants, many of whom are veterans in the hospitality industry at such places as the Ritz Carleton and Sandals Resorts. These hires appeared to solve their problem of being shorthanded when college students return to school in the fall. However, the Jamaica experiment didn't pan out as well as The Shepler team had hoped. After one year, the Shepler team decided to make a strong effort to address the seasonal availability challenge they face with part time student help by hiring local students, retired folks looking for full time employment and others that are available for the full season.

Smoking and drinking are discouraged during off hours and are strictly forbidden on the job. Drug use at any time results in immediate action. Bill Shepler points out, "All new hires are automatically drug tested, and everyone knows that random drug tests can be announced at any time." Legal drugs must be accompanied by a doctor's prescription. The Coast Guard mandates frequent drug and alcohol testing for anyone working on the boats. Some people are surprised to learn that Shepler's doesn't automatically fire a crew member who fails the drug test.

Bill says, "Our attitude is: 'How can we help you?' We try to get that person into a rehabilitation program. Of course, anyone who refuses help can't work here." In actual practice, drug users usually quit before being tested.

Once hired, the new worker goes through a training program. Must-read literature includes a brief history of the company, detailed descriptions of all the jobs, and an outstandingly comprehensive explanation of company policies. The employee manual spells out every aspect of work for every employee at all times. Attorney Ellen Crane, who spent summers working at the ferry service, checked out every aspect of the entire manual.

A two- day training session called "Shepler's Traditions" is held at the Grand Hotel on Mackinac Island in the months of May and June. At that session, Bill Shepler discusses the Shepler traditions, heritage, and culture. He relates how the company has grown and delves deeply into the Shepler culture. Bill feels strongly that every employee must understand and embrace the culture in order to be a part of the team. During his lecture, Bill often sounds like the successful athletic coach he once was.

The group breaks for lunch in a private Grand Hotel dining room, giving crew members a chance to get better acquainted and enjoy the hotel. The Grand Hotel is rightly famous for its food. During the next part of the training session, Chris narrates a PowerPoint presentation of nuts and bolts issues such as benefits, policies, responsibilities, and rules. He also shows the smart and practical uniforms Shepler's people wear at all times: a variety of shirts, pants, jackets, and raingear suitable for all kinds of weather. Crew members are expected to buy their own uniforms (at half price) and keep them neat and clean. Although it may seem to be a minor point, the importance of wearing a name tag correctly is strictly enforced. The Shepler Logo is on the left side of the front of the shirt and the employee name tag is to be placed on the right side, lined up evenly with the Shepler logo. The name tag is placed on the right side to accommodate the fact that when an employee shakes hands with a guest, the guest will be looking at the employee's name tag.

A Visit to Mackinac Island

Interstate I-75 leads to Mackinaw City. Take exit 338 and follow the signs. At the big Shepler's sign on the gateway at the dock, you'll be met by a greeter who will ask if you'll be parking for the day or overnight. Day parkers are sent to the nearest parking lot. If the main lot is full, you'll be told how to get to a satellite lot, where a tram will be waiting to take you back to the dock. If you're planning to stay on the island overnight, you'll go out to the unloading area to drop off your luggage and select the kind of overnight parking you prefer. Shepler's provides three types of overnight parking: an open, free outdoor lot, a lighted and fenced outdoor lot, and spaces inside storage buildings. They also offer Drop Off Service that will take your car to any of the three lots. More and more guests are choosing Drop Off Service. You can buy your ferry ticket and select your parking area at the ticket office, but a lot of guests will have bought their tickets and made their parking choices online before they even start their trips. You can also buy online tickets for carriage rides and Grand Hotel lunch and admission tickets.

Shepler's longstanding service policy is to take care of all of the customer's needs, efficiently and effectively, so that all the customers have to do is enjoy the ride and the forthcoming island visit. The basic idea is that there should be no worries and no troubles, even for first-time visitors who don't know what boat they are getting on, how their luggage gets to their hotel, how their car is safeguarded, and a host of other concerns. Shepler's takes all of these worries off the table.

If you want to tour the island by bicycle, you can rent one on the island or take your own with you on the ferry. The 8.5-mile road around the island offers great views of the Straits, the Mackinac Bridge, the Upper Peninsula, and Lake Huron.

While you're waiting for your ferry, coffee, cold drinks, snacks, and sunglasses are available at Captain Bill's Espresso and Coffee Bar. Film, T-shirts, umbrellas, and raincoats are also available. You won't have a long wait; a ferry leaves hourly during the shoulder seasons (spring and fall) and every half hour during the busy summer season. As you board, you'll be met by your captain and the deck crew. Deck hands put in part of their hours on the docks, where they greet guests, tag luggage to be taken to various hotels, unload cars, and load luggage carts. When on the boat working as deck hands, they report directly to their captains. They make sure the vessel is clean and ready to go and assist the captain in leaving the harbor and docking. They load and unload luggage, strollers, and bikes, collect tickets, and help passengers. They learn line handling, docking, knots, and basic navigation. They're also trained in first aid and learn how to respond in possible emergencies. All of Shepler's captains, including Fleet Captain Billy Shepler, started out as deck hands. If you need help or have questions, just ask a deck hand. They're trained to know the answers.

Welcome on Board

Today, your captain is Erik Heffernan. He looks so boyish, it's hard to believe that he's been driving ferries since 1999. Like all of Shepler's captains, he's thoroughly experienced, has passed the comprehensive Coast Guard exams, and is licensed to operate the ferry under Admiralty Laws. He'll tell you about today's wind and water conditions, describe what the motion of the vessel will likely be, and let you know if you're likely to get some spray on the top deck. The view from up top is spectacular. The enclosed main deck lounge has wide aisles and cushioned seats that are a little more comfortable than top-deck seating. It will take about sixteen minutes to reach the island.

As the vessel leaves the harbor, you'll be told where life jackets are located and reminded that eating, drinking, and smoking are not allowed on board. It is foggy, so Captain Erik will make two or three security calls during the crossing to let other vessels know where we are and where we're going. He has adjusted the radar screen to his liking. It pinpoints just where other vessels in the area are and also shows what kind of weather is coming.

He explains that every captain has his own way of adjusting the radar and driving the boat. Erik tells us that when there's fog, the water's calm unless the wind is from the east.

There's a wonderful view of the breathtaking

Mackinac Bridge. If you're on one the Mighty Mac Departures, you'll be treated to a close-up, under-the-bridge trip on your way to the island at no additional cost. It includes a narration of the history and building of the bridge. School groups can request the bridge detour by asking in advance. A member of the deck crew passes among the passengers with Mackinac Island guidebooks for sale.

Erik, like all the captains, is fascinated by the weather. Yesterday was a day of pea soup fog, bright sunshine, and "blacker than black" thunderstorms. "Everything but snow," says Erik. "Before I got this job, I never paid any attention to the weather; now, first thing in the morning, I turn on the weather channel." Erik makes about ten or eleven crossings a day, working from seven thirty a.m. to eight p.m., six days a week.

As you make your way to Mackinac Island, you pass the 1894 Round Island Lighthouse. The building was automated and its keepers removed in 1922. It was replaced by the automated Round Island Passage Light in 1948, which you pass as you make your way into Mackinac Island Harbor.

According to lighthouse cruise narrator Terry Pepper, "Four of the eight sides are adorned with huge bronze medallions depicting the face of an Indian chief. Many believe the medallions depict the face of Chief Petoskey; however, they are actually generic representations installed by the Coast Guard to honor the rich Native American tradition of the Straits area. As the eastbound lighthouse cruise passes the light, Bill Shepler sometimes jokingly takes the microphone to point out that his research has revealed that the busts actually show Chief Running Water, who had three famous sons, Hot, Luke, and Cold. Terry also says that since 1970, the old Round Island Lighthouse has undergone extensive repairs and restoration by a dedicated group of volunteers.

You enter the harbor between the east and west break walls. The *Felicity* has come in from St. Ignace, and the captains exchange greetings and weather information. Being able to talk to other captains is one way to relieve stress. As the ferry enters the harbor, Erik points out places of interest: the Grand Hotel, Fort Mackinac, and the Michigan Governor's House. He tells guests how to get to the visitors' center and reminds them to remain seated until the vessel is secured and baggage is unloaded. "Don't forget to gather up all your belongings and hold on to your children," he adds.

A few steps down the ramp and you're on Mackinac Island. It's a place with a long and colorful history. Native Americans, who inhabited it at least since 900 AD, regarded it as a sacred place, home of the Great Spirit or Gitche  Manitou. As such, it was a gathering place for tribes and the holy place where chiefs were buried. They called it Michilimakinac. Some scholars say that means "place of the dancing spirits," and others claim it means "swimming turtle." Still other scholars say both names are fables.

Arch Rock was an especially important site to the Natives. According to tribal lore, it was the bridge over which departed souls went to their final resting place; it's a place that inspires great awe. Even the bravest of the Odawas refused to walk on it. Geologists tell us that the 149-foot limestone arch was formed during the Nipissing postglacial period.

The highest point of Mackinac Island is Fort Holmes, the remains of a British fort. It is 320 feet above lake level. The island can only be reached by ferries, small aircraft, and private boats and by snowmobiles in the winter.

The first European to visit the Straits was French explorer Jean Nicolet, who came by canoe in 1634. At the time, a huge part of North America was claimed by the French, and they were already established in Quebec and Montreal. Nicolet was followed by French missionaries who came to convert the Indians and are said to have brought along lilac bushes. That may or may not be another fable. W. Stewart Woodfill, longtime owner of the Grand Hotel, claimed to have made up the story. Fable or not, the island has been famous for its lilacs since 1949. Mackinac Island holds its annual Lilac Festival in early June. According to the American Bus Association, the Lilac Festival is one of the nation's top hundred tourist attractions. You can see over one hundred varieties of lilacs in some unexpected colors like blue, yellow, and magenta. Some of the bushes have grown as big as trees. Besides enjoying the flowers, festivalgoers can join in a 10K race, wine tasting, and street dancing and can watch musical performances, the crowning of the Lilac Queen, and the nation's largest all-horse grand parade. There's also a fundraiser called the Feast of Eponi, named after the goddess of horses and protector of all animals.

Horses play an important role in the Mackinac Island scene. Motorized traffic was banned in 1898 after carriage drivers complained that the new horseless carriages spooked the horses. Now, all vehicles are horse-drawn, with the exception of bikes, firefighting equipment, emergency vehicles, and construction equipment. M-185, which circles the island, is the nation's only state highway without motorized traffic or a stoplight. Three hundred huge Percheron and Belgian horses pull the island's carriages, taxis, and freight drays. The horses each work half-day shifts and typically live to be about thirty years old. In the fall, most of them are taken by boat to winter quarters in the Upper Peninsula.

Climb aboard the Mackinac Island Carriage Tour to see the island. The horses clop past souvenir, gift, and camera shops and some of the seventeen fudge shops. In 1887, Newton Murdick opened the island's first fudge shop, using his mother's recipe. Now, the Island's one million yearly visitors, somewhat affectionately known as "fudgies," consume about ten thousand pounds every day. Favorite flavors are chocolate, chocolate walnut, peanut butter pecan, vanilla pecan, crème de menthe, and maple. The annual Fudge Festival is celebrated in late August.

Today, fudge is Mackinac's most important product, but Europeans originally came to the island to buy furs. At the time of Louis XIII and Louis XIV, big fur hats were the rage of the Continent. They were made of a felted mixture of wool, adhesive, and beaver fur. New France was full of beavers. France's wily Cardinal Richelieu encouraged the fur trade, planning to use it as a way to build stronger colonies in the area. The Indians brought their furs to Mackinac Island from all over the Great Lakes and Canada. It was conveniently located for travelers to stop and get supplies. French—and then British—traders bought the furs for guns, cutlery, beads, blankets, vermillion paint, and whiskey. One beaver skin would buy four charges of powder or shot or as much vermillion as the tip of a knife would hold. Soon, the beaver hides, trimmed and stretched to a circular shape, became the standard medium of exchange. One skin was called *abiminikwa* by the Indians and by the French. It wasn't long before the British joined in the fur trade and took it over completely after the French and Indian Wars. To the British, Mackinac Island was "The Gibraltar of the Great Lakes," a strategic military post as well as a prosperous trading center.

In 1808, New York entrepreneur John Jacob Astor established his American Fur Company on the island and eventually became the number one name in the fur trade. He named Robert Stuart as his Mackinac Island manager. Stuart and his wife, Elizabeth, became social leaders of the little community and built Stuart House to entertain their many guests. Although imposing in size, architecturally it's a simple nineteenth-century building.

Other architecture on the island reflects the tastes and backgrounds of many generations of people who have called Mackinac home. The majority of buildings are designed in Victorian styles: Italianate, second empire, Richardson Romanesque, and stick style, but the island offers three hundred years of architectural history, including Native American, colonial, federalist, and Greek revival. Mackinac Island also has the only example of northern French rustic architecture in the United States. Fort Mackinac is a European adaptation of Islamic architecture. The fort was built in 1781 when the British, fearing another Indian attack, deserted Fort Michilimackinac on the mainland and moved to the island, which they bought from the Chippewa Indians for five thousand pounds. They never wanted to give it up to the Americans, and ownership went back and forth during and after the War of 1812. The Americans took permanent control in 1815. Today, the fourteen original buildings have been restored, and costumed interpreters portray soldiers and civilians from the 1800s.

Another early building is the Mission Church, which was built in 1829 as the first Protestant church on the island. It's the oldest surviving church in Michigan. The Indian Dormitory was built in 1836 as a place for

Indians to stay when they came to collect government funds owed them. It was also used as a school. The dormitory was restored in 1966 and turned into a museum. Mission House, built in 1820, was a boarding school for Indian children. It was turned into a hotel in 1849 and became a rooming house in 1939. Restored, it's now used as quarters for state park employees. Mackinac National Park was established in 1873 as America's second national park, just three years after Yellowstone became the nation's first. When the federal government left in 1895, the park became Michigan's first state park. Today, the park has demonstrations of hearth cooking and crafts and has a working blacksmith shop. The annual Benjamin Blacksmith Convention takes place there in early August.

The state park is also the site of the Beaumont Memorial, named after Dr. William Beaumont. He was an army surgeon stationed at Fort Mackinac in 1822 when a Canadian trapper named Alexis St. Martin was accidentally shot in the stomach. Dr. Beaumont stitched him up, but when the wound healed, St. Martin was left with a window in his stomach. Beaumont recognized a great opportunity to learn about digestion. In the following years, he conducted experiments and observed through a plastic window that covered the opening, how long it takes various kinds of foods to be digested, how gastric juices work, and even how emotions affect the stomach. He published his classic work, *Experiments and Observations on the Gastric Juice and the Physiology of Digestion*, in 1833. Royal Oak's Beaumont Hospital is named for him. To date, nothing has been named for Alexis St. Martin, who got literally fed up with the experiments.

Michigan governors have been luckier. They enjoy a summer residence on the island with a great view of the harbor. In 1929, young Gerald Ford was one of the first Eagle Scouts chosen by the state park commission as honor guards for Governor Fred Green. In 1975, he returned for a two-day visit. His helicopter landed at the Eagle Scout barracks, but the president stayed in the Grand Hotel.

The famous Grand Hotel Old Summer Inn was built in 1887 by the Michigan Central Railroad to encourage people to travel to the North Country on its trains. The hotel is famous for its 667- foot porch, the longest in the world. So many people want to see it up close that the hotel now has to charge admission to enter the grounds. The Grand Hotel was the setting for two movies. In 1946, *This Time for Keeps* starred Esther Williams, Johnnie Johnson, and Jimmy Durante. The Esther Williams Pool was built at that time for her swimming scenes. In 1981, *Somewhere in Time* starred Jane Seymour and Christopher Reeves in the story of a man who went back in time and found his true love at the Grand. The film has become such a classic that every year, fans come to the island for a costumed weekend recalling the romance of the movie. The Grand has 385 rooms, no two alike, and originally appealed to wealthy Eastern socialites eager to trade their hot cities for Michigan's cool breezes. When the advent of air conditioning made the island less desirable, its hotels began to appeal to conventions. Today, those conventions range from Michigan Republicans, who gather to discuss affairs of state, to the Red Hats, whose motto is "Girls just want to have fun." The Grand has numerous meeting rooms equipped with all the latest audiovisual equipment. It also has a world-class golf course.

Mission Point Resort was originally built in the fifties and sixties by Frank Buchman as headquarters for his International Moral Rearmament Association. Since then it has been extensively remodeled to handle meetings, banquets, and conventions. It has wireless Internet, audiovisual facilities, handicapped access, and a variety of meeting rooms plus spa services, a health club, and a pool. It has 242 rooms including 92 suites.

All in all, the island has a combination of forty-six hotels and inns, plus bed-and-breakfast spots. Many have long histories. The oldest, The Island House, has been in operation since 1858.

The Harbor View Inn was once the home of Mackinac's legendary Odawa-French Madame LaFramboise. When her husband was murdered in 1806 by a disgruntled Indian, she took over his fur-trading business and made a success of it, even though buying and selling furs was strictly for men back then. When Ned Wickes stayed at the Harbor View with his grandmother back in the 1930s, he was more interested in the nearby Coast Guard lifeboat station. "Every morning, a bell would ring, the boathouse door would flip open, and a fully-manned boat came down a steep track and hit the water with a splash. What a show!"

The Iroquois Hotel dates back to 1902 and is located right on the harbor. Next-door Windemere Beach is the scene of the annual Stone Skipping Contest put on by the Gerplunketing Club. The present professional record is thirty-three skips.

The Chippewa is another historic hotel, first built in 1901. Its Pink Pony Bar is a favorite watering hole for the yachting crowd who flock to Mackinac in July. The island is the terminus of two of the nation's longest and most prestigious fresh-water sailboat races. The Port Huron to Mackinac race attracts well over two hundred entries, and the Chicago to Mackinac race has more than four hundred, ranging from modest sailboats to maxi-yachts. The Port Huron marked its eighty-fourth run in 2008, and that year, the Chicago race celebrated its centennial with a fabulous display of fireworks over the Straits. At the end of each race, there are parties all over the island.

Shepler's Champions

In the early years of their marriage, Bill and Suzanne moved to Aspen, Colorado, to enjoy its skiing opportunities. Both of them waited tables at the Jerome Hotel, but Bill soon found a job more to his liking. He was hired as a member of the ski patrol.

In 1958, Royce Asher came looking for ski instructors to teach skiing at Boyne Mountain. Bill accepted the job offer. As a ski instructor, Bill worked first under Royce Asher and later under Stein Erickson and then Othmar Schneider. Shortly thereafter, he was appointed an examiner of ski instructors. Two years later he became the head ski examiner for the central division of the Professional Ski Instructors of America (PSIA), covering a sixteen-state area. This winter career meshed perfectly with the ferry business, which took up the rest of the year.

Bill was assigned to the new area that Boyne Mountain had just completed. This ski area is known as Boyne Highlands. Bill had twelve instructors working under him. Dick Babcock was one of them. Dick describes Bill as "one of the prettiest and most accomplished skiers I have ever seen. He was a perfectionist and a hard task-master, but I enjoyed working with Bill and knowing him. On Sunday afternoons, Bill would often get the ski school folks together to show off a bit. One of four drills was to ski in a single line, very close together, doing very tight turns almost in unison. Bill also had the uncanny ability to stop almost instantly. One time he did that when an unusually large instructor, Jack Frank (a.k.a. Smoky the Dancing Bear), who weighed about 250 pounds was right behind him. Bill stopped, Jack yelled 'No, Bill,' and then groped him in a bear hug, and they both tumbled down the slope."

Bill created a venture he called "Captain Billy's Ski Cruise" to teach skiing in the Rocky Mountains. For about ten years, Bill would enlist groups of nineteen people to spend a ski week in the soft snow of Colorado, combining fun with a variety of experiences that taught balance, control, and safe navigation while turning, skiing over moguls, and dealing with deep snow. The first year, he took his recruits to Vail. After that, he took them to his friend Bob Elkin's ski resort in Steamboat Springs. Each year, he took three different groups during the months of December and January.

Bill Crane shares the following story about his experience with one of those weekends: "I joined a group going to Bill's school at Steamboat Springs. After a morning of instruction, Bill took us to the top of the slope where we stood overlooking the large pine trees below. 'Ve vill follow me,' he would say. Then he would shoot down the steep, deep hill covered with powdered snow. We were instructed to follow him and copy exactly what he did. He challenged us to try things we never in our right minds would have done. But because he was Bill Shepler, we followed him. The snow beneath the trees was held up by the branches, so the hollow under the tree was covered with only a shallow layer of powdered snow, which, of course, accelerated our speed. Once we passed under the branches and through the hollow, we were really flying. As we exited the area beneath the trees, we suddenly plowed full speed into a huge, chest-deep wall of powdered snow. To Bill's shout of 'powder puma,' we would create an explosion of snow. A tree branch grabbed my hat, and I came to a stop with my goggles askew and one goggle full of snow. My fellow skiers were all in a similar state, disheveled but thrilled with the fact that we had survived the challenge. Bill had the ability to challenge people in ways that opened up whole new worlds of possibility and action—both in teaching skiing and in running Shepler's Mackinac Island Ferry Service. That was Bill—he was a great teacher who loved to blend learning with fun and adventure. Every night we celebrated with hot fudge sundaes."

Dick Babcock added: "Ski weeks were very popular then. Our students would come on Sunday, have lessons every day, and leave on Friday noon. Every Friday afternoon we'd have an instructor's clinic. We'd go over everything that happened during the week and critique each other's teaching. Bill liked to have us all on the same page so we would all teach the same techniques and methods. We mostly taught the Austrian technique. Our staff was a combination of Austrian and American instructors."

Bill himself loved to play hockey. He used to get the instructors into hockey games on the pond at the entrance to the main lodge at the Highlands. Often these were international competitions between the Austrians and the Americans. Among Bill's ski students at Boyne were members of the Detroit Red Wings Hockey Team, including Gordy Howe, Marty Pavlic, and Ted Lindsey.

Bill's career ended at Boyne for what Dick Babcock thinks were mostly political and cultural reasons. "A guy named Othmar Schneider took over as director," he says. "He leaned very strongly not only toward Austrian techniques but also to the Austrian culture. It went so far that a German accent was very desirable."

Bill, who was now serving as the chief examiner for the Central Ski Instructor's Association, went to a Sun Valley ski symposium with several ski examiners. Ski examiners determine who qualifies as certified ski instructors.

On his flight home, Bill had a unique experience that truly affected his thinking about customer service. Bill tells the story of what happened: "After the Sun Valley outing, we boarded a 727 out of Boise to go home. For a few minutes, the pilot and I talked about flying. I spent years in the air force, so I was familiar with planes and flying. One feature of the 727 was a door in the rear. We left Boise and landed in Salt Lake, taking on a full complement of passengers. At 35,000 feet, the back door started to leak. I'd spent two thousand hours in the air, but this is the first time I ever sweated blood. I knew that the unequal pressure would cause the tail assembly to go. The flight attendant moved passengers from the back to the front, and I thought, 'A lot of good that's going to do them—the whole plane is going to crash'. The pilot dove ten thousand feet. All the babies on the plane were screaming because their ears hurt. I felt like screaming too, but I didn't. We finally got stabilized and landed safely. Unbelievable relief! One and a half hours later, we got the announcement that our plane was boarding for Detroit—and it was the very same plane. As I was boarding I thought, 'Why am I doing this?' One hundred other passengers did the same thing. We were all a bunch of mindless customers." The point Bill is making is that Shepler's wants customers to fully realize the safe situation they are in while traveling on a Shepler's Ferry boat.

In 1975, John Deschermeier moved back to northern Michigan. Bill had certified John when Bill was the chief ski instructor and chairman of the central division for the United States Ski Association. By 1975, Bill was free of those responsibilities, so John was excited about telling Bill about a plan he was developing. He hoped that Bill would share his enthusiasm for the idea and join John in his efforts to bring the idea to fruition.

In essence, John told Bill that he felt that there was a need for a ski program dedicated to advanced ski racers. He did not want this program to compete with ski schools and high school ski programs. He also didn't want the program to be a for-profit venture.

Bill loved the idea, and he and John formed a board of directors consisting of John as president, Bill as vice president, Jack Frank as secretary/treasurer, and Tim Parsons and Greg Smith as at-large board members. They named their company the Northern Michigan Ski Academy, wanting to convey that it would serve a broad area and endure long after the current members stepped aside.

The board set the Northern Michigan Ski Academy up as a nonprofit, 501(3)(c) organization. The group developed a mission statement asserting that the academy was not a "learn to ski" endeavor. Rather, its purpose was to help each individual racer to personally advance to the best of his or her ability. There was no "Win one for the Gipper" intention for this program.

The Northern Michigan Ski Academy opened in 1978 and unfolded in two phases. The first phase was designed to ensure that each of the coaches was thoroughly competent at teaching and coaching. The second phase consisted of marketing and advertising this program. The first class had twenty young participants. To qualify for the academy, participants had to already know how to ski, be able to get on a ski lift without help, and be able to be away from their parents for a couple of hours at a time.

Bill and John found a great site for their teaching and coaching when Jim Dilworth, general manager, offered and provided total cooperation. According to John Deschermeier, "Any reasonable request was enthusiastically endorsed and supported by Dilworth."

John went on to say, "Within five years, we grew to 150 participants, and after ten years we were serving four hundred racers. We were growing so well that in 1987 we opened a second branch of the academy at Boyne Mountain. Through the academy, we were developing young ski racers who were greeted with open arms by the high school ski coaches. The coaches benefited from this great feeder program, which is still producing great ski racers at Nub's Nob and Boyne Mountain. Bill was my hero. Whenever I had a question on my face, I would go to Bill. He has always been a great listener, a great coach, and a great friend."

One day, George Menzi, principal of Harbor Springs High School, contacted Bill. The ski teams were not doing well, even though Harbor Springs lies nestled among three great ski resorts. Bill became the coach for the Harbor Springs High School ski teams. His girls ski team won the state championship in Bill's eighth year. This was Harbor Springs' first state championship in any sport. It was the first time a class-D high school ski team had defeated class-A and class-B teams, which represented much bigger enrollments. For instance, Traverse City's team had 180 members. Harbor Springs had only 25 kids on its team. Bill's ongoing success was rewarded when he was elected to the Michigan Ski Coach's Hall of Fame.

Bill was a strict disciplinarian who demanded a lot from his team members. Playing for Bill, you didn't smoke, and you didn't miss practice. Bill says, "I had a rule that if you missed practice you couldn't compete in the next meet." He adds, "In the month of November prior to the ski season, I organized a 'dry land training program' to condition the team. They practiced running on the school parking lot, in the halls, in the cafeteria, up and down the stairs, and so on. Every night we ran for five miles, and I ran with them. I never asked them to do anything I wouldn't do myself." Bill is still that way. Trainees are sometimes surprised to see the CEO of the company out on the dock, unloading luggage and parking cars.

Through his coaching, Bill realized that even though Harbor Springs was located in the middle of a prime ski area, there were children who didn't have the opportunity to learn to ski. He worked with the Kiwanis Club, the city, and Jim Dilworth to develop a program to teach all area students from first grade through sixth grade to ski. The program became a part of Shay Elementary School's physical education curriculum, and it didn't cost the taxpayers a dime. This got started when Bill went to Principal Tom Richard with a proposal to incorporate ski instruction into the curriculum. Tom Richards accepted Bill's offer to teach Tom's students for no salary, and the Kiwanis Club made ski poles, boots, and skis available to each student.

To make all of this work, Bill needed volunteers to help. Bill would teach the skiing, but he needed parents to help put skis on, pick up kids who fell, recover lost poles, help the kids get on and off the rope tow, etc. About eight or nine parent volunteers with kids in the program showed up every day. Each class, grades one through six, spent two hours skiing per day for three days over a period of two months.

To really help these kids, they needed a good beginner's hill. Bill, Dave Irish and Dick Babcock discovered an old dump site that had about a 150-foot vertical drop. The city agreed to cover the hill with dirt and agreed to use their packers to work in packing the snow. Jim Dilworth had engineered the new Boyne Highlands ski lifts, and he agreed to design a simple motor-driven rope-and-pulley system to get the kids up the hill. In addition to donating skis, poles, and boots, the Kiwanis Club built a warming house at the top of the hill. This collective effort produced a feeder system for Harbor Springs. It was called the Shay Elementary Ski Program, and it operated with the support of Principal Tom Richards.

When Principal George Menzi had originally asked Bill to coach the Harbor Springs High School ski teams, Bill had agreed to do it for one year. His one-year agreement stretched into eight years, and he was followed by his sons Chris and Billy. "Chips off the old block," they also coached championship teams. Chris coached eight years, producing one boys' state championship (with Billy as his assistant coach), and then Billy went on to coach for six years, producing six more state championship teams. These guys know how to produce winners! Billy Shepler was quick to give credit to the great feeder system that brought talent to the high school ski teams throughout the northern Michigan area.

When he was twenty years old, Billy took time off from the ferry business and worked in Harbor Springs as a windsurfer instructor in the summer and a ski coach in the winter. He remembers it as a great, carefree time, but when he was twenty-two, he came back to the family business and earned his captain's license. "Dad seemed happy to get me back," he says simply.

Although Chris played three sports in high school and coached the 1996 state champion boys ski team from Harbor Springs High School, his most impressive sports achievements came in a completely different area. Racing sailboats has been his passion since he was ten years old. By 1985, he was racing in the Southern Ocean Racing Conference in Florida and in a lot of Great Lakes competitions. In the fall of that year, just before his last year at the University of Rhode Island, he got a phone call from sailing legend Harry "Buddy" Melges. He had been named "Yachtsman of the Year" three times and won more national and world titles than any living American, including an Olympic gold medal in 1972.

Melges was known also as a skilled boat builder and sail maker. The first time he raced Star Class boats, he met Dennis Conner, who was a well-known Star sailor. Conner looked at the homemade sails and said, "It's too bad you have to sail with your own sails."

"Well," said Melges, "we'll just have to have a go at it and see what happens." Melges went on to win the series without having to race the last race. Melges asked Conner afterward, "Would you like to borrow my sails to race the last race? I know the guy who makes them, and I can get you a good deal!"

Chris had sailed with Melges's daughter Laura, running the bow on a J-35 class yacht in little day races around northern Michigan. She liked what she saw and recommended Chris to her dad, who was starting an America's Cup campaign.

The America's Cup is the world's oldest continuous sporting competition and the most prestigious race in yachting history. The first race was run in 1851. The competitors were the New York Yacht Club and the Royal Yacht Squadron.

In 1985, when Chris got his call for a tryout for the Heart of America team that would be racing in the first freshwater race in Chicago, he was overjoyed. Recalling his excitement, he said: "I was supposed to finish classes at the University of Rhode Island in two weeks, but when you have a dream this big it reduces everything else to rubble." Chris was serving as a captain for Shepler's at the time, and fleet captain David Sullivan allowed him to go. His dad, however, was not happy about Chris taking time off work. Chris proposed a toast to himself at a family gathering, saying, "I have a tryout with the America's Cup team!" No one joined the toast. Chris said, "I slammed my wine glass down and left."

The first day of his tryout, Chris stayed at a Super 8 Motel. When he arrived at the Chicago Yacht Club at Monroe Station, Chris said, "I saw this tall, bent mast, swept back. In those days, having a mast that had that much rake was a big deal. I parked my diesel Volkswagen. I was shaking. I was going to step on a boat I had dreamed about sailing for twenty years. I was feeling like an NFL player who takes his first steps on the field and hears the roar of the crowd."

Chris was quickly brought back down to earth. As soon as he stepped on the boat, he was met with, "That winch needs cleaning!"

Chris was kept in suspense as to whether he would make the Heart of America team. "After seven days of sailing, I was never told to stay or go. By Sunday, I was out of money and clean clothes. That last day, we sailed all day. Upon returning to the dock, we saw the United States Women's Sailing Team standing there. They were all beautiful ladies, and there I was, going home. As I told them I was going home, I hoped they would tell me to stay. When they said, 'Go ahead,' I figured I was out. Even if I had been cut, I had sailed with Buddy Melges, Bill Shore, Charley Scott, and Gary Jobson (current ESPN announcer and three-time America's Cup winner) and others."

Chris got home early Monday morning, completely exhausted. The next morning the phone rang, and Suzanne answered. She calmly said, "Chris, it's America's Cup on the phone." Sharon, a British lady who ran the shore guide operations, was on the phone. She said, "Chris, we want you back. Your ticket is at the Pellston Airport. See you tomorrow." Chris still had no sure idea of what was to come.

The Heart of America had purchased the *Clipper*, and Chris and the others trained on it across the United States. "We held lots of fundraisers up and down the contiguous shorelines out of Chicago. As November arrived, it got cold, so we sent the Clipper to Victoria, British Columbia. We got twenty-four inches of snow there, but we learned a lot about our crew and boat speed.

We trained against the boat *Canada II*—all straight lines, five hours on one tack. I got frostbite. We were testing all kinds of technologies, evaluating straight-line speed and sail trim."

After many hours of training with *Canada II*, the Heart of America leadership decided that *Clipper* was not good enough to compete in Australia. Heart of America started a new design. The *Clipper* was taken to San Francisco, where the team met up with *Canada II, True North,* and *Pacific Telesis*. According to Chris, "We all trained together, but *Pacific Telesis* had all of the studs: Paul Cayard, Tom Blachaller, and others."

During a month off, Chris went to Florida to sail with the Southern Ocean Racing Conference on a boat named *Mustang*, from the Netherlands. Ken Reed was the director of the program. When Chris returned to San Francisco for training, he met people he had read about. It was truly thrilling.

Chris shares, "In San Francisco, a fundraiser was held in the Oakland Estuary. *Pacific Telesis* arranged the race to raise money. We kicked their ass! And we did it in front of all the big donors on the dock. Buddy Melges stole the show and got money that would have gone to *Pacific Telesis*. People loved Buddy's personality. We stayed at the Marriot on Fisherman's Wharf. I felt like I was living the life of a professional athlete. In many ways we were professional athletes, being paid seventy dollars per week.

"We launched the new boat in May of 1986. Once we decided it was ready to go, I still didn't know for sure if I had made the team. People came and went. In the summer of 1986, we moved the boat to Santa Cruz, California. Because of the Santa Anna winds (ten to thirty knots of breeze), it was much like what we could expect in Australia. We trained with *Canada II* from May through August.

"In mid-May the cuts started coming down. Guys I had been with for the past sixteen months were given their walking papers. I got the call from Buddy. I knew this was it. I wasn't the best or the strongest, nor was I the worst or the weakest. My top quality was being a really good team player."

Buddy told Chris, "You made the team." Chris knew he had to keep it to himself, but he felt like yelling it from the rooftops.

The Louis Vuitton trials were held during October, November, December, and January. The Heart of America finished sixth in the world. Stars and Stripes beat Kookaburra, bringing the title back to the United States. The America's Cup experience was clearly a highlight in Chris's life. It was amazing how well he had handled the uncertainty around whether he would make the America's Cup team or not. His ability to tolerate uncertainty would be of great value when he got his chance to take over the reins of the Shepler's Mackinac Island Ferry Service.

Survive and Advance

by Don Steele

As I thought I was nearing the end of my consulting period that was designed to help the Shepler family transition ownership and operations of its business from the second to the third generation, a crisis arose like a sudden storm on the Straits of Mackinac. The very survival of Shepler's Mackinac Island Ferry was at stake. All thoughts of Bill's retirement were shelved, and he and Chris committed to investing whatever time, energy, and money it took to save their livelihood. This wasn't the first time Shepler's had to fight for their survival since Cap founded the business in 1945, but it clearly emerged as the most serious challenge.

It all began when Petoskey attorney Jim Wynn came up with a plan to create a monopoly ferry service by somehow consolidating Arnold Transit, Star Line, and Shepler's into one ferry service operation, under his ownership. Wynn knew that the Brown family was considering selling Arnold Transit and some premier properties. He would need to purchase the Brown family docks and other properties if he were to accomplish his mission. He would also have to negotiate deals with Star Line, Shepler's, and the island city council.

The Brown family's influence in this northernmost region of Michigan began with Michigan's beloved senator Prentiss Brown. Prentiss had played a critical role in the building of the Mackinac Bridge that united the Lower and Upper Peninsulas of Michigan. The patriarch of a large family, he was also an astute businessman who fostered a diverse and successful family enterprise. Over the years, the Browns acquired, among other things, the Arnold Transit Company and premium real estate constituting half of Main Street on Mackinac Island and several prime properties in St. Ignace and Mackinaw City.

The Brown family had decided prior to 2010 to offer its business and property assets for sale. This sale became a reality on June 22, 2010, when the Browns sold Arnold Transit, their docks, and other prime properties to Jim Wynn. Wynn was able to consummate this deal by securing very substantial help from The Great American Life Insurance Company. This Cincinnati-based company provided a first mortgage against all of the assets Wynn had secured from the Browns for an undisclosed price, as reflected in eighty-nine pages of legal property descriptions and security agreements recorded with the Register of Deeds on June 26, 2010.

The sale was difficult for the Brown family. The *Detroit News* reported on August 14, 2010, "Sale of Mackinac ferry service splits family: After 90 years of ownership, an outsider had taken the helm." The article further revealed, "Jim Brown had mixed feelings. A third-generation owner of the Mackinac Island ferry service, Arnold Transit Co., Brown wanted to keep the business in the family. But he could see that other members felt differently." Brown added, "It didn't mean as much to some of them."

While the possibility of selling had been debated for years, the debate came to a head, pitting one generation against another. "My generation wanted to sell," said former Arnold Transit CEO Paul Brown, the youngest of the second-generation owners—but that's how it goes. Whoever has the votes carries the day. It's like an election—you win or you lose. In the end, we're all fine with it."

The Sheplers soon learned that Wynn had big plans. In a closed-door meeting with the Mackinac Island city council on August 11, 2010, Wynn had offered to sell the docks that Arnold Transit used on Mackinac Island, Mackinaw City, and St. Ignace to Mackinac Island for an undisclosed price and then lease them back from the city. This negotiation was reported by Mayor Doud at the city council's next meeting, held on August 24, 2010. Jim Wynn's big plan included his creating an "exclusive franchise" as opposed to the current "nonexclusive" franchise agreements that were currently in place.

Dan Musser, president of the Grand Hotel on Mackinac Island, reflected on his initial thoughts when he learned about Wynn's proposal to the City of Mackinac Island: "Jim Wynn is a compelling guy, gregarious and charming. In addition to being an attorney, he has an accounting degree." Then Dan added, "When I first heard about Jim's business model idea, I knew that the Brown family was interested in selling Arnold Transit. Wynn's plan might be a case of great timing. In essence, Jim's plan was to buy Arnold Transit and bring Shepler's and Star Line under his Arnold banner. My initial feeling was that if he could do this arguably his business model could be good for all parties."

The mayor and the city council appeared to be enamored with Wynn's proposed business model. Mayor Doud reported at the August 25 city council meeting that the Mackinac Island city council had met in executive session on August 11 with Jim Wynn. She said, "This is a rare opportunity, and we intend to further pursue this matter and determine the benefits that would be provided to the city. It is one way that the City of Mackinac Island can secure that we will always be protected in having property to run a boat line if and when the city ever needed to."

Bill and Chris Shepler, however, saw Wynn's business model very differently. It looked to them as if Wynn was trying to create a monopoly. When Bill and Chris refused to sell, Bill said, "Wynn threatened to drive us out of business." They feared that they might lose their entire business, without just compensation. The very large mortgage the Sheplers had incurred to modernize their vessels with energy-efficient, cleaner engines could not be paid off if the business failed to survive. The banks would call in their loans, and the 180 people employed by Shepler's would be out of their jobs. Shepler's could face bankruptcy

The Sheplers were galvanized into action. Their response was swift and certain. They requested a nonexclusive franchise from the Michigan Public Service Commission (MPSC) and the Mackinac Island city council while also challenging the authority of the Mackinac Island city council to grant the exclusive franchises Wynn was seeking.

Additionally, they communicated directly with bankers, group tours, convention groups, and other large group customers that would be negatively impacted if Shepler's didn't survive the Wynn challenge. On the legal front, they hired Ed Koester, a nationally respected attorney from Naples, Florida, the local attorney Ellen Crane, and Al Ernst, a specialist in regulatory law. To examine the facts concerning the benefits and liabilities of a monopoly ferry service, they hired a world-class economist, Henry Fishkind. The city council had indicated that they planned to hire an economist, but they never did. Fishkind interviewed business people in all three cities and concluded that a monopoly would have negative consequences—with the probable exception being Jim Wynn. Finally, they hired one of Michigan's prominent lobbyists, Pat Harrington, to communicate with the then-Governor Granholm, the House of Representatives, the state senate, and the attorney general's office.

While Shepler's was working to save its business, someone else was galvanizing others into action. Marketing and social media consultant Ami Woods (a resident of Good Hart, Michigan) created a pro-Shepler's, anti-monopoly Facebook page that was designed to gather opinions and facts. Posts would mostly consist of news articles, memorandums, and other documentation. Excerpts from such documents were captioned. Ami never posted an opinion of her own, and her Facebook effort was not sponsored in any way by Shepler's.

Ami had this to say about her Facebook initiative: "I first heard about the single-franchise debacle from Chris Shepler in late September 2010. I was shocked. How was it possible I hadn't heard that all this was going on, right here in my backyard? Immediately I wanted to help. My concern was that if I was in the dark on the situation, likely many others were as well. My family was in the dark. I asked friends; they knew nothing. Associates knew nothing. Industry leaders knew nothing. I was terribly surprised to learn that all this politicking was going on; an attempt was being made to shut out a sixty-year-old family business in small-town America, and so few people knew. It wasn't news, but it needed to be just that. The situation needed a public voice. Being a marketing and media consultant, a friend of the Shepler family, and a lifetime visitor to Mackinac Island, I felt that a logical way to assist would be to harness the power of social media.

"On September 24, 2010, I launched a Facebook page to promote awareness on the issue (still active as of March 14, 2014 at http://www.facebook.com/stoptheferrymonopoly). The page had over a hundred users in just twelve hours. After twenty-four hours had passed, the number rose to three hundred. Within three days, there were 673 active users—150 more people than Mackinac Island's population. Within thirty days from launch, over two thousand active users were present, and at peak, over three thousand users from all over the world were visiting daily, weighing in on the issue, stating opinions, and showing support for Shepler's Mackinac Island Ferry.

"The page attracted users from across the United States and beyond, including the United Kingdom, France, Jamaica, and as far away as Thailand. Of the three thousand–plus users, less than eight hundred were from northern Michigan. More than fifty users had Mackinac Island listed as their current residence—approximately 10 percent of the island's population.

"Paid 'Likes' and Facebook advertising didn't exist at the time. The users were organic; they were merely everyday people from all over the world who very much opposed the single-franchise system and who were against what the Mackinac Island council was attempting to do.

"The FB page was an amazing effort that informed users of meeting dates, letter-writing campaigns, interviews, updates, etc. It was a gathering place, a meeting spot, an instant and immediate source of information on the issues as they happened. Meeting coverage was posted in real time on the FB page, including the October 20 and November 3 meetings. Users were present from all over the world, posting over 150 comments per meeting.

"Most importantly, what the FB page brought to the surface was that this issue was not a matter of local politics. It wasn't just impacting a local business and a tiny island in northern Michigan. It was impacting the memories of literally thousands of people around the globe who very much opposed what Mackinac Island was attempting. And once those people were in the know, they were not shy in voicing their opinions."

On September 29, 2010, Ami Woods wrote an open letter regarding the Mackinac Island ferry situation, addressed and stated as follows:

> Dear Mayor Doud:
>
> I was born and raised in northern Michigan. My family's livelihood depends primarily on tourism in this beautiful area we are all fortunate to call home. I worry that you and your council members have not properly analyzed the potentially devastating outcome of the situation.
>
> While I learned today via a local newspaper that you had not read the letter from the Michigan Chamber of Commerce, I hope you will take the time to read mine.
>
> This situation has two very delicate, different sides. I am not referring to the sides of those involved. I am referring to those affected—our community and our tourists.
>
> On the one hand you have the potential dirty politicking, the alleged back-office dealings, the possible job loss affecting hundreds of northern Michigan families that may happen if a monopoly is allowed. Those are the tangible, immediate issues that will cause a serious stir locally and leave a pool of bad blood in the aftermath. What is more devastating is the regional public relations disaster that has already begun to unfold in the past week.
>
> You have been graced as mayor of an island which, as an attraction, is one of the top tourist destinations in the Midwest. I hope you have enjoyed the love and affection so many had for your area, because I fear that your actions

have changed how the world views Mackinac Island. For your sake and the sake of so many employees relying on a successful summer season on Mackinac Island, please think carefully about each move you make.

You're no longer just pushing the buttons of local businesses and politicians. You are also pulling the heartstrings of literally millions of tourists who enjoy a very special part of their Mackinac Island experience—the ferry ride.

"Come and take a ride, it's fast and it's fun" … "The rooster tail" … "Catch the cat." All three phrases bring a positive sentiment to different people for different reasons. Your council is ruining those sentiments with your actions. Personally I ride Shepler's. The bright blue and white awnings, the friendly dock attendants, and the hassle-free experience in general are my own personal gateway to Mackinac Island. I have participated in countless class trips to the island. I've enjoyed numerous scout outings, memorable day trips with my grandparents, my Sweet Sixteen dinner, girls' weekends during college, professional conferences as an area businesswoman, and even a recent memorial for a dear friend, at his dying wish—all via Shepler's. The memories generated from these trips are similar to those of other folks who have visited the island for so many years.

Quite bluntly, Mayor Doud, I don't want you, your council, or any other form of government screwing with my memories. I hope that you will soon answer the call of so many reaching out to you and end this political circus by renewing each franchise agreement. I am not in favor of a monopoly, and I certainly do not want to see any family business forced out of business by local government.

Thank you for your time.

Yours sincerely,
Ami Woods

On the legal front, Koester advised Shepler's that Wynn's creation of a monopoly would be in defiance of the Sherman Antitrust Act, the Michigan Antitrust Act, the Michigan Ferry Boat Code of 1921, and its own city ordinance. He also pointed out that a seizure of Shepler's business, even in effect by government regulation, without just compensation, is specifically forbidden under the Fifth Amendment of the United States Constitution. Judge Emeritus Bill Crane further explains, "Most people think of the Fifth Amendment as it relates to self-incrimination. However, the last clause of the Fifth Amendment prohibits a government from taking your property without just compensation, which is the very cornerstone of the free enterprise system." This last clause states, in part, "Nor shall private property be taken for public use without just compensation."

At the September 24, 2010, council meeting, the council asked the three ferry boat lines to submit new proposals for their franchises. These proposals were to include the rates, schedules, and "property proposals." Due largely to this added request for property proposals, the Sheplers filed a federal district lawsuit on October 4, 2010. On the same day, Shepler's requested a continuation of their nonexclusive franchise from the city council. Wynn's new entity, Northern Ferry Company, which included Star Line and excluded Shepler's, was requesting an exclusive franchise. The city council meeting to hear these proposals and comments from the public was scheduled for October 20, 2010. For the hearing on October 20, Bill hired a certified public court recorder to transcribe all of the proceedings. The city hall was overflowing with concerned citizens. The first presenter was Jim Wynn.

Jim Wynn's Proposal

Jim Wynn, from the beginning, had made it clear that he wanted an exclusive franchise. Making that happen would require consolidating or eliminating the existing competition. In support of his monopolistic plan, Wynn proposed the following benefits to the council: "What consolidation does, is it allows (us) to reduce fares across the board. It allows us to reduce freight charges across the board. We are enabled to expand service. We can have more boats at different times not only during the season but in the shoulder seasons as well. We could have—ultimately we could have year-round service if the city would like to explore that."

As an additional enticement, Wynn offered the following: "Consolidation would also allow the Arnold Transit and Star Line combined company, Northern Ferry Company, to pay the city a greatly increased fee. Right now, the city currently collects the franchise fees from all three franchises. The franchise fee is in the range of about $300,000. Our proposal is that we would go from $300,000 to a minimum of $1,200,000 in the form of a franchise fee up to $2,700,000 in a franchise fee to the city. And in that franchise fee, the city could be—it would enable it to use revenue bonds to purchase critical pieces of real estate, if that's what the city would like to do, against revenue bonds on the lease-back from the ferry boat company, not on the back of taxpayers. It's a revenue bond."

Wynn's statement verified, in the collective minds of the Shepler family, that Wynn's intentions were to sell the docks he had purchased from the Browns to the island, thereby enabling him to pay off all or most of his first mortgage to Great American Life Insurance while still retaining the rest of the prime property assets he had acquired in his deal with the Browns. Wynn could then rent the docks back from the city for use by his ferry line.

To further quote Wynn, "The intent is never to put anyone out of business. The intent is to fix the system, to improve the service to the island and help the island. That's the entire intent."

In answering questions from the city council members and the floor, Wynn seemed to contradict his earlier statement about not trying to put others out of business. An audience member asked, "Is there a way this can go through and Shepler's remains in business?"

Wynn responded, "The efficiencies we propose with the reduced rates, reduced freight costs, and the increase in the franchise fee can only work with a single franchise. That's the only way to go about it."

Shepler Attorney Ed Koester's Letter of Response

Attorney Ed Koester, in his letter to the island council dated October 19, 2010, stated the following: "I understand that a meeting has been set for Wednesday, October 20, 2010, for the City of Mackinac Island to hear twenty-minute presentations on the proposals submitted to the island on October 4, 2010. As you are aware, Shepler's has contested from the outset the alleged proposal process and has explained to the island council that under applicable law, the island does not have the right to grant monopolies or require bidding or proposals for franchises. The island is facing very real liability for acting outside the scope of its authority. The announcements by island officials that the island is considering a monopoly to Shepler's competitors have caused significant financial damage to Shepler's. The island has wrongfully denied Shepler's proper application for a franchise."

Koester then added, "There has been a lot of discussion regarding the applicable law in this matter, and yet the island has never provided anything but the vaguest of generalities to the effect that the island can simply do as it sees fit with the ferry business. With the island and its officials on the brink of again violating Michigan law, I request that the island actually respond and explain the alleged legal authority for causing damage to Shepler's and waiving the potential of granting or denying a franchise, as though it is a magic wand to be used at the whim and caprice of the island's officials."

According to Koester's letter, the island's actions were violating its own ordinances; Sec. 66–94 under the city's ferry code states, "Any franchise issued pursuant to this article shall be a nonexclusive franchise for a term of not to exceed twenty years." Even more damaging, the city's charter specifically prohibits the granting of exclusive franchises, as set forth in Chapter IX, Section 1: "But no exclusive rights, privileges or permits shall be granted by the Council to any person or persons, or to any corporation, for any purpose whatever."

"In addition," Koester wrote, "Shepler's has now been asked to provide information in support of a new application on something never requested before, to wit: 'property proposals.' Property proposals are a subject which has no bearing on the criteria set forth in the Ordinances. Shepler's can show that James F. Wynn and Arnold Transit Company have already combined and taken action to restrain trade in the relevant market, including with respect to Star Line.

"Michigan law has long recognized a municipality has no inherent authority to grant an exclusive license, permit, or franchise unless the state legislature explicitly and expressly grants that exclusive right, which they did not. In the instant case, the city council of Mackinac Island has acted arbitrarily and capriciously by failing to approve Shepler's application for a nonexclusive franchise for ferry boat service. There is no valid reason why the city council of Mackinac Island should deny Shepler's application, because Shepler's has met all of the required criteria under the ordinances.

"Wynn's threats to ruin Shepler's through his efforts to receive a monopoly from the city to put Shepler's out of business is in fact a clear violation of the actual text of the applicable laws. Quoting from Section 1 of the Sherman Antitrust Act: 'Every contract, combination in the form of trust or otherwise, or conspiracy, in restraint of trade or commerce among the several states, or with foreign nations, is declared to be illegal. Every person who shall make any contract or engage in any combination or conspiracy hereby declared to be illegal shall be deemed guilty of felony, and on conviction thereof, shall be punished by fine not exceeding $100,000,000 if a corporation, or, if any other person, $1,000,000, or imprisonment not exceeding 10 years or both said punishments, in the discretion of the court' (15 USCA Section 1). And, Section 2 of the Sherman Antitrust Act states: 'Every person who shall monopolize, or attempt to monopolize, or combine or conspire with any person or persons to monopolize any part of the trade or commerce among the several states, or with foreign nations, shall be deemed guilty of a felony, and, on conviction thereof, shall be punished by fine not exceeding $100,000,000 if a corporation, or, if any other person, $1,000,000 or by imprisonment, in the discretion of the court' (15 USCA. Section 2).

"The regulation of ferry boats has been preempted by Carriers by Water Act, MCL Sections 460.201–460.206. The Michigan Carriers by Water Act was enacted in 1921 and therefore came after the island's charter."

Shepler's Attorney Ellen Crane Speaks to the Island Council

Shepler's attorney, Ellen Crane, went into some detail about each of the allegations stated above when she addressed the island council during the October 20 meeting. According to Ellen, "First of all, the island is violating its own ordinances. Their request for proposal went far beyond what the ordinances require. The ordinance says that the applications for a franchise should include the applicant's name, the principal place of doing business and description of the ferry boat, (and) the scheduled ferry boat services. And upon approval of the schedule and service and upon receipt of an application fee, the council shall issue a franchise. This is not a discretionary matter. They meet the minimum requirements. You shall issue that franchise. It is to be, according to your own ordinance, a nonexclusive franchise. Consideration of an exclusive franchise violates your own ordinance."

Furthermore, "The second point made in that letter is that the city does not have the authority within its charter to grant monopolies. Michigan law has long recognized a municipality has no inherent authority to grant an exclusive license, permit, or franchise unless the state legislature explicitly and expressly grants that exclusive right. If you look at your charter, you do not have the explicit right to grant an exclusive franchise."

Ellen Crane then added as a third point. "Some of the statements today bring concerns about the third point brought up in this letter. The Mackinac Island council's arbitrary and capricious behavior is unlawful. Asking for an open-ended proposal on things such as property, or such as us proposing franchise fees to you, opens doors to all kinds of different considerations. And there seemed to be some statements made today that made me concerned about the extent of your dealings with one of these private ferry boat providers. The fact is that there are antitrust law violations that have apparently already occurred. That law not only prohibits creating monopolies but also prohibits engaging in a conspiracy. For every person to otherwise engage in is a conspiracy, to engage in a discussion is, in fact, prohibited by those antitrust laws. And those are felony violations that carry up to a million-dollar penalty for individuals who engage in those conversations and up to a hundred million for corporations that engage in that behavior."

Attorney Ellen Crane then concluded her remarks with the following observations: "Your claim that you can regulate the rates of the ferries is, in fact, governed by the Michigan Carriers by Waters Act, MCL Section 460.201–460.206 of 1921, and that's a specific point addressed in this letter. I think Shepler's, I think the island residents, and I think that the business community deserves from the island what its position is. And rather than making blanket statements to the press, give us some authority. We went through an extensive amount of research to determine these things, and they're serious matters to Shepler's, who are facing losing their business from this activity that's already occurred."

"Finally I want to make a point of clarification on the *Arnold Transit v. Mackinac Island* case that was finally returned in 1984. The sole issue determined in that case is that Mackinac Island has the right to generate revenue from the franchise fee. It is not the blessing to govern rates, schedules and all other things that have been represented by others when they discuss this case. Furthermore, it wasn't taken up by the US Supreme Court. The US Supreme Court was appealed to, and they said, 'No, we don't want to consider that.' They let prior rulings stand. So that case is not a source of authority for you to go far beyond setting franchise fees which are revenue for the city. I urge you to consider granting Mr. Shepler's application for a twenty-year franchise."

Attorneys Cavanaugh (for the City of Mackinac Island) and Ettinger (for Arnold Transit) offered denials of the accused violations spelled out in Ed Koester's letter. It was suggested that the issues brought to bear by Shepler's attorneys would be settled in court.

Bill Shepler's Presentation of Shepler's Proposal

While the theme of Jim Wynn and Tom Pfeiffelman's presentation to the council was essentially, "the system is broken and we can fix it," Bill and Chris Shepler took a very different approach. In essence, they focused on reviewing the history of the franchise that Cap Shepler had started in 1946. Bill started the speech with, "I don't know why I'm here. I don't know why you're here." They took people on an emotional journey covering much of what the Sheplers had been through in building and sustaining their business for sixty-five years. In Bill's words, "So to make a long, long story short, we've ended up with five specially designed hydroplane boats that service you folks and the people visiting the island, we think, with the best possible service to the island. That's our aim, that's our goal, that's our legacy, that's our challenge. All due respect to our colleagues that state they are running at a sixteen-percent capacity; we're running at a seventy-eight-percent capacity. Further our fuel consumption is at seventeen-hundred-dollars a day as compared to our competitors at twenty-five-hundred dollars a day. So you see, our system is not broken." He then added, "Now, we've applied for a franchise for twenty years three times. And I'm sure we'll be refused again tonight. If I have to wait to March to make sure I got a franchise, what do I do between now and March? And I may not have a franchise. I've got—as Tom says, we've got tons of debt out there. I've got bills to pay. What happens to my crew? Do they have a job, or are they going to be laid off? So that's the need for a franchise—a twenty-year franchise. A twenty-year franchise allows any good businessman to plan, budget, and project what's going to happen in the next five, ten, fifteen years. Do I build a new boat? Do I buy more property? Do I refurbish? Do I redesign? All of these things go into our budget plan each year. And if you're in business, you know what I'm talking about."

Bill continued, "And the domino effect of me going out of business. I'm sure you've considered that. I hope you considered that. Shepler's lease their Mackinaw city dock from the Village of Mackinaw City, which is 12 percent of the Mackinaw City budget. Thus the taxpayers will be affected; it affects Mackinaw City, St. Ignace, and this island. I've got 180 employees that depend on me for livelihoods. Some have kids in college, some are paying for cars, some are paying house rents—the list goes on and on and on. They depend on their job working for this tiny company called Shepler's Mackinac Island Ferry. I want to protect those people, as all of you want to protect them. That's why I'm here."

Bill Shepler went on to talk about capacity, scheduling, fares, money spent on new energy-efficient engines that ensure less pollution, refurbishing Shepler's boats, and other issues of concern. Then Bill turned to the monopoly issue. In his words, "The monopolistic effect will have a devastating effect on Mackinaw City and St. Ignace as well as Mackinac Island, in spite of the charts you've been looking at. Yeah, we like to compete. We think it's great. Somebody said, 'Would you do this all over again?' Yeah, in a heartbeat. The impact on visitors, the impact on conventions, and the impact on large groups—we got some people in the audience. We want people to have the choice, as I think everybody in this room would like to have the choice."

Bill closed his presentation to the Mackinac Island City Council with this: "I have a little side note. We received an e-mail and a picture of a family that visited us a couple of days ago. And you really can't see it. But here's a family with our cast members saluting the flag on our dock. And, of course, the e-mail was just outstanding—the fun they had on the island, how they enjoyed their visit, the service they received from our staff. It was all so positive. We don't want that to go away. I'm pleading for my life right now. I'm pleading for our very existence. All I want is a twenty-year franchise. Thank you for your time. I thank you for coming regardless of which side of the fence you are on. Thank you for being here. Thank you for listening."

There was a moment of silence, followed by an explosion of clapping and cheering. It took several minutes before Mayor Doud was able to restore order.

Dick Moehl, who was prominent in the saving of the Coast Guard cutter *Mackinaw* and was at that time president of the Great Lakes Lighthouse Keepers Association, said to the council, "What are you doing to a fellow man that had trust in America? To think they spent their money to upgrade their vessels, and this to serve you people on Mackinac

Island—folks, to me, that's absolutely wrong. There's something wrong with this idea."

Another audience member said, "Everyone here did the Pledge of Allegiance before we sat down. And I think the comment was liberty and justice for all. I don't think that's the case in this meeting." Not one person spoke on behalf of Jim Wynn.

Of special note, at a subsequent island council meeting, convened on November 17, 2010, Councilman Barnwell introduced island resident Jeff Shaffer. He lauded Shaffer for taking time to review, categorize, and recap all 295 letters received by the council. Upset to learn that the city council members had not read the letters, Shaffer took the time to make a difference and brief his results. Shaffer consolidated the input into a thick packet available to each Council member and to audience members. Shaffer noted that the letters came from 106 cities, crossing two countries and twelve states. In all those, Shaffer said, there was "Not one letter for Arnold to get their franchise at all."

At that same meeting, the city voted to issue two year, nonexclusive franchises to all three ferry boat companies, yet failed to spell out the terms and conditions. The city did not issue the twenty-year franchise agreement according to the previous terms. In a press release dated November 22, 2010, Chris Shepler stated, "The city's earlier attempt to create a monopoly on ferry service by granting just one franchise was at least temporarily scuttled amid a firestorm of opposition this fall. Opponents include island residents, area businesses, the Michigan Chamber of Commerce, and the prestigious Bay View Yacht Club that conducts the very popular Port Huron to Mackinac Island sailing race."

Following the November 17 Mackinac Island council session, and after Shepler's learned that it would not be granted a twenty-year nonexclusive contract, there was a paper blizzard of motions by attorney Ed Koester asking for various reliefs. In light of the council's discussions about wanting ice-to-ice service, Shepler's resumed ferry boat service in mid-November and gave discount tickets. Island residents could buy year-round service for a mere $75.

Ed Koester sent a letter dated October 11, 2010, to each potential defendant, giving formal notice to "Preserve all evidence related to the lawsuit which has been filed against you. Litigation has commenced and you are not to manipulate, change or destroy any evidence in this case including, without limitation, e-mails, documents, files, correspondence, submissions, applications, proposals, photographs, videos, computer backups, including tapes or any data related to the lawsuit."

Early in November 2010, the city police issued four citations against Shepler's and served them on Chris Shepler in the pilot house when he landed on the island. After getting the four citations, Shepler's discontinued service and offered full refunds for the season tickets.

According to the *St. Ignace News*, "Four citations issued by the City of Mackinac Island to Shepler's Mackinac Ferry were dismissed by Judge Richard May, representing the 92nd District Court in Petoskey Monday, March 21, 2011. Shepler's press release said, "This charge was dismissed, and Chris was found innocent of all charges."

Chris Shepler issued a press release that states, "First and foremost, we will make good with all of our devoted customers. Shepler's simply wants the opportunity to continue providing them with the island's premier ferry service." He further states, "We appreciate the unwavering support of our customers and are committed to making sure they are not inconvenienced by the city's action."

Also on March 21, 2011, Judge Dennis W. Mack ruled that the City of Mackinac Island's authority to regulate the ferry boats is preempted by the Michigan Public Service Commission. That decision has never been appealed and thus has the force of law. Chris Shepler's press release further stated, "Shepler's Mackinac Island Ferry respects Administrative Law Judge Mack's ruling today that the Michigan Public Service Commission has authority to investigate and regulate the rates, fees, and other charges that are set for the ferry companies serving Mackinac Island and dismissed the City of Mackinac Island's claim that the city alone has that authority! Clearly, this issue has far-reaching implications for the state and local economies."

Because the island never approved a non-exclusive franchise including all terms and conditions, there was a hearing scheduled before Federal District Judge Neff, requesting that the ferry boats be allowed to operate under the terms and conditions of the previous franchise agreement. An agreement was reached for the years 2011–2012 in Judge Janet Neff's court in Grand Rapids, Michigan, on April 12, 2011. Pursuant to this, Shepler's signed a voluntary dismissal of the federal lawsuit "without prejudice" and without costs. While the terms and conditions of the two-year franchise were confiscatory, the Sheplers felt they had no choice but to accept these confiscatory terms and conditions because at least they allowed them to continue to operate. The issue of "an exclusive (monopoly) franchise" was not discussed again.

Unfortunately, the battle did not end there. All three ferry lines got into financial difficulties because of the confiscatory terms of the city's franchise agreement, which included requiring the ferry lines to operate ice-to-ice (at times when there were virtually no visitors going to the island) and nearly tripling the franchise fees. As a further complication, Jim Wynn, in his ongoing efforts to drive Shepler's out of business, lowered his rates from the approved rate of $24 to $22, forcing Shepler's and Star Line to do the same. Wynn had all of the rents from the premier properties he had purchased from the Browns to subsidize his ferry boat business.

On August 24, 2011, Ed Koester sent a letter the island attorney, Michael E. Cavanaugh, challenging the legality of the nearly tripled franchise fee of 7 percent. Koester stated, "The franchise fee is unreasonable because it is a substantial increase over prior years and over $1 million is excessive for any unidentifiable costs and expenditures. Because the 7 percent franchise fee is unreasonable, it violated the Mackinac Island Charter." Then, Koester reiterated, "The franchise fee is arbitrary and capricious. The City Council decided on 7 percent with no apparent reasoning to support their decision other than the amount was less than the highest amount offered (Jim Wynn at 9%), an arbitrary decision that should not withstand scrutiny." Koester goes on to cite Michigan cases to say that a decision is considered capricious if it is 'apt to change suddenly, or is freakish or whimsical.'

Koester sent a copy of the Cavanaugh letter and a draft letter to Governor Rick Snyder to arm lobbyist Pat Harrington with additional legal arguments. In his proposed letter to Governor Snyder, Koester wrote, "I humbly request that you ask Attorney General Bill Schuette to issue an opinion resolving the dispute regarding the legal rights of the respective parties to regulate ferry boat service." Ultimately, it was resolved that new legislation would be the better solution to resolving the issues.

After the island continued to fail to provide relief or respond with any legal authority to justify the confiscatory terms to the franchise requirements, new legislation was drafted to affirm the state of Michigan's preemptive power to regulate ferry operations. Over several months, draft legislation was worked on by legislative and administrative authorities. It was apparent to all that the ferry companies could not afford the confiscatory terms of the franchise agreement. Almost no passengers were visiting the island on the mandated ice-to-ice schedule. All three ferry companies requested relief during the fall and winter.

During the first year of operations under the Mackinac Island city council's new rules, Shepler's suffered a decline of $1.2 million in gross revenue. This loss was due to a combination of the council's rule changes and the increasing costs for fuel. Shepler's were forced to run nine hundred trips over and above the schedule they had planned to run. Each departure cost about $300 for staff and fuel, not including things like depreciation. Bill and Chris could only assume that Arnold Transit and Star Line lost revenue also.

The Sheplers also appealed to newly elected governor Rick Snyder, Senate Majority Leader Randy Richardville, Speaker of the House Jase Bolger, Attorney General Bill Schuette, and other legislative and administrative officials. The island continued to turn a deaf ear to the ferry boat companies' pleas for financial relief. By early January, 2011, it became apparent to everybody that relief was not forthcoming, and without intervention from the Michigan government there might be no boats to carry passengers among Mackinaw City, St. Ignace, and Mackinac Island in 2012.

In May 2012, after seven months, and twelve rewrites, in a concerted effort to eliminate the island's control over the ferry boat industry servicing the island, two bills hit the Senate floor (SB 1150 and SB 1151). The bills were drafted in cooperation with the attorney general's office, the Michigan Public Service Commission, and the governor's office. In essence, these bills would enable Shepler's to retain their nonexclusive franchise free of the city's confiscatory regulations.

While all this was happening, Dan Musser, president of the Grand Hotel, and others were becoming more and more skeptical of Jim Wynn's ability to put all of the pieces together to achieve his plan. These folks were also acutely aware of the recent negative publicity and the potential damage such publicity could cause to the northern Michigan tourist trade. This was of special concern because at the same time, Michigan was spending millions on its "Pure Michigan" campaign to promote the northern Michigan tourist trade.

Dan Musser had this to say: "When Wynn was unable to generate concrete agreements with Shepler's or Star Line and the state senate was about to hear and probably decide on the two pro-Shepler's senate bills, many of us got concerned. The coverage in the media of all that was happening could have negative effects on the tourist trade and the overall image of Mackinac Island, Michigan's number-one tourist attraction. Perhaps more importantly, I, along with others, hold the belief that, for the most part, the rules of engagement of the free enterprise system should determine the fates of these independent ferry services. Our position was to let the boat lines, rather than the city or state government, set pricing and schedules in response to customer needs, wants, and demands. The boat lines need passengers to survive and generate profits. In my thinking, if one fails, so be it! The others will survive and move on. At Grand Hotel, we are going to continue to need passengers, freight food, mail, etc., and so will the other island businesses."

Musser then added, "By the time the state government got involved, we had a more complete picture of Wynn's situation. It appeared that his quest for a single ferry service operation had lost momentum. With the Grand Hotel being the biggest business, the biggest user, and the largest taxpayer, I was probably best positioned to bring all of the key players together in an attempt to resolve the situation locally. My basic thought was, 'If the government can resolve the problems that they have during the Policy Conference, why can't we [Mackinac Island] solve this?'"

Finally, Musser revealed, "I worked with lobbyist (and chairman of the Michigan State Park Association) Dennis Cawthorne to pull all of the key players together for what turned out to be a two-day meeting at the Grand Hotel. Attending this meeting were the following people: Bill Shepler, Chris Shepler, Jason St.Onge, Dennis Cawthorne, Linda Pfeiffelman, Tom Pfeiffelman, Carol Rearick, Dan Musser Sr., Dan Musser, Jim Wynn, Bob Brown, Brad Chambers, Bill Chambers, and Margaret Doud.

During the somewhat contentious first day, Friday, June 5, Bill was conspicuously quiet until Dan Musser asked what he thought. Chris looked at Bill and said, "Go for it, Dad." Bill looked around and the room with a slight smile, looking each person at the meeting in the eye. With the room completely quiet, he stated, "I want everybody in this room to know that as of this moment, Shepler's Mackinac Island Ferry will no longer be controlled by the Mackinac Island Council. From this date on, Shepler's will set their own fares. Shepler's will also determine their own scheduled departures. They will determine what time of the day they start and end their departures, and they will determine the dates they start and end their service for each season. Now that you have heard our position, if further discussion is warranted, both Chris and I are willing to listen." Bill sat down to stony silence for twenty seconds before conversation began again. His point was made and ultimately, the group drafted an eleven-point memorandum that detailed what could be done to resolve the continuing conflict before the senate voted on the bills, taking the decision out of the hands of those most affected. Doing this would avoid a raft of publicity that could negatively affect the northern Michigan tourist industry.

The Sheplers bought into Musser's strategy because it was consistent with their philosophy. Attorney Ellen Crane addressed the island council, as reported in the *St. Ignace News* on January 20, 2011, in reference to the council's plan to use its perceived regulatory power to mandate ice-to-ice operations by all ferry lines. Shepler's was opposing this regulatory action, and Crane spelled out where the Sheplers stood on this and other council-mandated regulatory issues. "One of the fundamental premises and philosophies that Shepler's has is, 'Let the market dictate what service is needed.' You have proposals here, and it looks like at least some of what ferry boats' assessment of what the market needs meets the island's expectations. And, of course, Shepler's prefers that there is as little government interference with the free market as possible. So, if there is a problem with what we've determined the free market demands, point out what additional problems there are. Then let us respond to that based on your knowledge of the Island's demands. Make it a constructive dialogue rather than a regulatory, government-dictated approach to it."

What Dan Musser was calling for and what Ellen Crane had previously clarified made perfect sense. And it worked! At the conclusion of two days of debate and negotiation, on June 6, a ten-point Memorandum of Understanding was unanimously voted on and passed. Mayor Margaret Doud strongly supported the Memorandum of Understanding, as did the Sheplers.

The headline in the *St. Ignace News* on June 14, 2012, read, "Island and Ferries Reach Compromise: Move Forestalls State Interference; 7% Franchise to End July 1." In the article, writer Matt Mikus reported the following: "With the threat of state interference, Mackinac Island City Council reached an agreement Wednesday, June 6, to modify its ferry franchise options for the next 15 years. Starting Sunday, July 1, the 7% ferry franchise on gross ticket sales will end, and the city will receive, instead, $600,000 annually from the three boat lines, adjusted annually for inflation. Ferry companies will be able to set their own rates and schedules, the Northern Ferry cooperative of Arnold Line and Star Line will be dissolved, and both companies will operate their own franchises. In addition, only one boat company will provide winter service; the city will no longer require all companies to make unprofitable runs, and the city will give $100,000 to subsidize whichever boat line operates in winter."

Moving forward, the competition between and among the ferry lines continues to be driven by the rules of engagement embedded in the free enterprise system that enables businesses to survive and advance (or fail) based on the merits of their performance on their field of play.

Shepler's latest battle for survival ultimately represents the American free enterprise system operating at its best. In the end, the problem was resolved by the parties most affected by the outcome. What began as a locally based battle escalated into a conflict that involved the governor, the attorney general's office, the senate majority leader, the speaker of the house, major lobbying groups, the president of the Grand Hotel, the president of Mackinac Island Carriage Tours, the Mackinac Island State Park Commission, the mayor and the city council, Jim Wynn, and others. As painful as it was along the way, in the end, the political process worked. It was "the court of public opinion, the residents, and the customers" that determined the outcome.

The conclusion of the monopoly case had a profound effect on Shepler's Ferry business and on the Straits as a whole. The outpouring of public support has made Shepler's the number one ferry line to Mackinac Island. This added business forces Shepler's to stay competitive, and it puts even more pressure on the company to strive to be the best in service, cleanliness, and speed, just as Cap wanted it in the beginning.

The Sheplers will continue to improve their business with projects like the retrofit on the *Sacre Bleu*, and the updated parking and ticketing systems. In 2015, they will once again be commissioning Moran Iron Works in Onaway, Michigan as they add to their fleet and introduce a new boat - the first new ferry boat for the business since Cap's namesake *Capt. Shepler* in 1986. It is quite a feat for a family to stay in business for this long, but the Shepler's have persevered through good old-fashioned hard work and commitment. That commitment is what has made their business and their family stronger.

Three generations...

Summing up all their years of trials and triumphs, Bill Shepler said. "When you stand for, and say the right things, and are truthful with your statements, and do what you say, you will eventually come out on top. We all can agree that this has been a tough climb, not only to survive but to win in the end." Undefeated.

Appendix

During his long and active life, Bill has received many awards and honors.

Bill served as an effective member on the chamber of commerce for over twenty-five years and was named man of the year of the Mackinaw City Chamber.

He received the Bob Everidge Lifetime Achievement Award, given at the 2004 convention of the National Tour Association, the global association for packaged travel. The award recognizes individuals who have made outstanding, ongoing contributions to the association, its members, and the industry as a whole. Bill was only the second recipient of the award in the history of the organization.

He was cofounder of Circle Michigan, an organization that promotes packaged travel in Michigan.

He was selected to serve on the National Tour Association's board of directors. and on the NTA Speaker's Bureau. The Speaker's Bureau provides experienced and knowledgeable speakers on tour and travel-related subjects. In 1995 Bill was elected as the chair of the NTA's Minneapolis Convention.

In 1986, he was appointed to the Michigan United Front, a liaison between the state and the tourism industry.

In 1992, he was appointed to the Michigan Tourism Commission and led a successful fight opposing pre–Labor Day school openings.

In 1996, he received the Distinguished Service Award from the National Tour Association.

He was a founder of the Michigan Chapter of the Destroyer Escort Service. He is a board member of the West Michigan Tourist Association. Governor John Engler appointed him to a second term on the Michigan Travel Commission. He was one of just fifteen recipients named an Ambassador of Tourism by Governor James Blanchard.

The Michigan Chamber of Commerce cited him for "leadership in the public interest."

The Disney Institute and the Michigan Travel Commission gave him the Mouscar Award "in recognition of your persistent, passionate enthusiasm for the Michigan Tourism Industry." The statuette was personally designed by Walt Disney, and only fifty were made.

Chris, following in his father's footsteps, is actively engaged in growing the Michigan tourism industry. Some of his activities include:

National Tour Association Board of Directors and Chairperson for the NTA convention in Detroit in 2005.

Pellston Regional Airport Air Service Task Force.

St. Ignace Visitor's Bureau, Board Vice-President.

Mackinac Island Tourism Bureau, Board of Directors.

American Bus Association, 2014 Marketplace Chairman.

American Bus Association Board Member.

Michigan Tourism Strategic Plan, Service Excellence Committee Member.

Citizens National Bank, Board of Directors.

Bibliography

Andrews, Roger. *Old Fort Mackinac on the Hill of History.* Leader Press: 1938.

Atwill, Willis, and Collins, Kreigh. "Did You Know? Michigan Centennial 1835–37." *Booth Newspapers:* 1935–1937.

Barry, James. *Ships of the Great Lakes.* Howell-North Books: 1973.

"Break the Ice: Visit the Mackinaw." *Northern Express Weekly,* August 2, 2008, May 19, 2008.

Burcar, Colleen. *You Know You're in Michigan When ...* Global Pequot Press: 2005.

Fornes, Mike. *Mackinac Bridge: A 50 Year Chronicle 1957–2007.* Cheboygan Tribune Printing Co.: 2007.

Havighurst, Walter. *The Long Ships' Passing.* Macmillan: 1945.Hyde, Charles K. *Historic Highway Bridges of Michigan.* Great Lakes Books: 1993.

Jobson, Gary, and Luray. Michael. *World Class Sailing.* Hearst Marine Books: 1987.

Kachadurian, Thomas. *Views of Mackinac Island.* Sleeping Bear Press: 2000.

Mackinaw Area Events Guide 2007. Mackinac Island State Parks Commission: 2007.

"Mackinaw Today 2008." Mackinaw Journal and Mackinaw Today: 2008.

Peterson, . *Historic Mackinac Island Visitor's Guide.* Mackinac Island State Park Commission.

Reigle, Rosalee. *Historic Women of Michigan.* Michigan Women's Studies Association: 1987.

Repplier, Agnes. *Pere Marquette.* Doubleday Doran: 1929.

Weeks, George. *Stewards of the State: The Governors of Michigan.* Detroit News and Historical Society of Michigan: 1987.

Acknowledgments

Friends and Family

David Armour

Dick Babcock

Jeff Beach

Bob Bordeaux

Noel Bufe

Frank Davis

Hap Dowle

Patrick Doyle

Ellen Eastman

Bob Fisher

Eleanor Jardino

Patty Janes, Ph.D

Rose LaPointe

Jack Kirby

Jerry Kramer

Stan McRae

Dick Moehl

Lisa Pallagi

Ray Rolak

Ned Wickes

Hal Williams

A special thanks to the leads and cast members of Shepler's Mackinac Ferry Service for their contributions of stories and anecdotes that add to this book.

Great Lakes Lighthouse Keepers Association

The Great Lakes Lighthouse Keepers Association has been narrating the Shepler's Lighthouse Cruises since 1985. The concept originated in the mind of Dick Moehl.